WIN YOUR HORSE'S HEART

and

BE A BETTER HORSEMAN

Sherry Jarvis

WingSpan Press

Printed in the United States of America

Published by WingSpan Press, Livermore, CA
www.wingspanpress.com

The WingSpan name, logo and colophon are the trademarks
of WingSpan Publishing.

Cover photo by Holly Phillipps, Burwell NE

ISBN 978-1-59594-289-0

First edition 2009

Library of Congress Control Number 2009921476

CONTENTS

CISCO: The Confidence Builder...............................135

Chapter 7 Time: Patience vs. Impatience

SUNSHINE: Prayers of Patience 163

POEM: *Meandering with Sunshine in the Shade* 175

Final Thoughts

Poem: Trail of Inspiration for the Journey 187

Excerpt from Robert Browning's "Paracelsus" 188

Summary

Recommended Resources to Further the Journey 194

Sherry with her Mom on one of her very first horseback rides

DEDICATION

"Opportunity is missed by most people because it is dressed in overalls and looks like work." -- Thomas A. Edison

This book is dedicated to my parents and husband who have always believed in me and encouraged me to be the best I can be. Also to all horse lovers who seek to be the best they can be and to all horses who hope their owners find some HORSE SENSE.

A man of kindness, to his beast is kind.
But, brutal actions show a brutal mind:
Remember, He who made thee, made the brute,
Who gave thee speech and reason, formed him mute;
He can't complain, but God's omniscient eye
Beholds thy cruelty - He hears his cry!
He was designed thy servant; not thy drudge,
But know - That his Creator is thy judge.

Unknown author from The Ladies'
Equestrian Guide, *1857*

ACKNOWLEDGMENTS

I am grateful to my husband for being patient with me during the long hours I have spent on the computer during this project. With his support I am able to follow my dreams. He is the one who does most of the chores to care for our herd of ten horses, so I can travel and live my passion to share with others. Without him I would not have the wherewithal to do what I do.

I will always be thankful to my parents who have encouraged me, from the time I could walk, to fly with eagle's wings, telling me I could be anything I set out to be. And my Dad who helped me edit this book, keeping me on track with suggestions and ideas. He made me examine my beliefs and think about what I feel and do in order to win a horse's heart.

I owe special thanks to all the horses I have had the opportunity to interact with, who have taught me about life and fulfilled me in more ways than I can describe. It is because of these equine friends I am so driven to share my passion with everyone. All horses deserve a chance to be their best and many are just waiting for the right person to come along who can win their heart!

I am forever indebted to the numerous instructors and horsemen who have taught me how to be savvy with horses. I learned up close and personal from some and with others from afar as I watched in silence and awe. I learned the right things to do from many of these horsemen and sometimes what not to do. There are other horsemen I never met but through their writings I have found answers to my questions.

The many students who have entrusted me to guide them on their horsemanship journey deserve acknowledgement as well, because they have taught me how to listen and be a better communicator. Every time I teach it helps me to become a better horsewoman. I am a student of horsemanship every day right along side those who put their confidence in me to help them and their horse.

There are more ideas and stories I wanted to discuss in this book than space will allow. If I were to share all the people and horses who have inspired, taught and helped me on this journey called horsemanship it would take more than one book. Even though I don't have room to mention every one of them by name, I hope to convey a message of gratitude to each one who has affected and enriched my life. They have helped mold me into the horsewoman and instructor I have become. Some of these influencers were not even horse people, but still they taught me many life lessons which I have transferred to winning a horse's heart. I must give credit where credit is due. I am who I am because of the people and horses (both positive and negative) who have given me the opportunity to grow and learn.

There may be just two kinds of horse people, those who love'em and those who don't. I am impressed by anyone who has a heart to win a horse's heart and even more so by those who find a way to allow it to happen. If this book helps more people do just that, then I couldn't be more blessed, because I have helped the ones I love, HORSES!

Sherry, Cisco, and Keith after a demonstration at NE Horse Expo

HORSES IN MY SOUL

As I recall the blessings from above,
My mind keeps repeating all that I love.

I have a good life even though I'm older,
I have goals and dreams which now seem bolder.

With a great husband, and a place to call home,
What more could one want, with a horse of my own.

Horses have always been a part of me,
Just like people, they're all different you see.

Like the song of a sweet turtle dove,
I give each one choices, kindness, and love.

My message is, with your horse you are free,
But what works for you, may not work for me.

It is trust we must develop each day,
Then play with'em, and give'em some hay.

A strong bond of trust builds great harmony,
As friends, we enjoy each other's company.

We both learn patience and a soft touch,
To us this means so very, very much.

My horse looks so handsome all dressed in his tack,
Small miracle, when he allows me to sit on his back.

Each successful ride without a trick or buck,
Should not be taken for granted, it isn't just luck.

To ride everyday until my lessons are done,
Before I pass on, we shall ride as one.

There's still so much I haven't learned,
To be called a horseman, it has to be earned.

Horses make me happy to be alive,
Through stresses and sadness, they help me survive.

Each one of my secrets they have faithfully kept,
So be kind and gentle, & full of respect.

Finally always remember their pride & dignity,
And develop the relationship with creativity.

–Sherry Jarvis 5-14-05

AUTHOR'S NOTE

Finding Feel

"You cannot depend on your eyes when your imagination is out of focus." -- Mark Twain

Many of you reading this are like me. You can't remember a time when you didn't love horses. No matter what style of riding, discipline, or competition we choose, in the end most of us want the same thing: A first-rate working relationship with a horse who is a willing and responsive partner. The way in which we go about achieving that goal may differ. But I have never heard anybody say, "I want to sell this darn horse because he is just too willing and responsive. We work together too well. He gives me his heart every day and he has become a part of me." No, instead, we cherish and esteem a horse like this so much that some people are even cloning them.

When a horse becomes a willing and responsive partner we know we have won his heart. But how do we do this? Is it even possible with every horse? I am going to present principles in this book which can lead to the kind of relationship where winning a horse's heart is possible. The closer I studied these principles the more I realized everything relates back to one imperative concept, which is *feel*.

But what is *feel*? And can we even define it? Could *feel* be defined void of a communication system based on clarity and understanding where a person has a great ability to show discernment and make quick decisions? Is it some kind of sixth sense or consciousness where the person has a deep awareness and perception of everything around them which causes them to give off a presence guaranteed to produce positive responses? Perhaps *feel* is profoundly related to emotions and the atmosphere one creates between two living creatures? Would it be conceivable that earned respect, trust and honesty are foundations of *feel*? Maybe *feel* could be described as a particular way of handling physical sensations like: touch, energy or a release which bring about harmonious and graceful movement? Does *feel* come from a belief system, a way of thinking, or a visualization of what is expected? I suspect that *feel* is so simple it seems complicated.

What is this thing horsemen call *feel*? When I ask this question of horsemen it is a concept they find hard to define. They come up with all kinds of vague descriptions which don't seem to capture the essence of true *feel*. I have yet to hear a clear definition which describes with accuracy the mysterious connection one sees when a great horseman displays true *feel*. It almost seems indefinable. Bill Dorrance and Leslie Desmond wrote a book on this topic. They describe it better than anyone else, but it took 376 pages to do it.

It is easier to see and experience *feel* than it is to read about it. When we watch people with horses it is pretty easy to see who has *feel* and who is having a hard time finding *feel*. True *feel* is very subtle and effective when done well. Without *feel* it is quite difficult, if not impossible to truly win a horse's heart, because it is the language he understands and can relate to.

Right now I am able to understand this concept of *feel* to a certain degree because of my combined experiences, education, and openness to continue learning. I am sure when I reread this book years or even months from now I will have a deeper understanding of the workings of true *feel*. In fact, from the day I started writing it two years ago my understanding and application of *feel* has been further developed and refined.   Finding *feel* is an evolutionary process for me. I wish I would wake up one day and be able to declare, "I have all the *feel* and understanding I need to win every horse's heart." Some horsemen may be born with it, like people say Bill Dorrance was. But for most of us it is a learning process.

In order to explain a small component of this concept of *feel* I will use an analogy from a personal story. A few years ago I injured my shoulder. My rotator cuff, bicep and triceps were all torn upon hitting the ground after being thrown from a horse. This injury taught me a lot about true *feel*.

Before the damage could be repaired through surgery I had to have physical therapy in order to regain some strength and range of motion. During this time I had two different therapists, one who was experienced and one who was just starting out. Both of them had the correct tools and knowledge but only one of them exhibited true *feel*. When I was handled by the therapist with true *feel* I felt confident and relaxed which caused me to be willing to work with him. I was more flexible when he manipulated my arm even though I could feel some tolerable pain. On the other hand, when I was in the hands of the fumbling therapist who lacked *feel*, I felt fear, anxiety, and even anger. This tension caused me to resist his movements. The consequence was intolerable pain and less flexibility.

As I reflect upon this experience I saw the relationship to a bit in a horse's mouth and hands which lack *feel* while holding the reins. I now have more empathy for a horse that is at the mercy of a human lacking *feel* even if he is equipped with all the correct tools and knowledge. It is not difficult to understand why a horse may be resistant when he is being banged and pushed around by a handler without precise *feel*.

I thought I knew what soft *feel* was from this experience. But it wasn't until after the surgery I discovered how little I knew about true *feel* and how subtle it really is. After the surgery, physical therapy was critical to my recovery. However, I had to travel over ninety miles in order to see the therapist who had *feel*. Other than the exercises the therapist gave me to do I was instructed not to use my arm for six weeks. Consequently my Mom had to drive me to the appointments. On the drive home from one of the appointments she asked me why I never told Bill, my therapist, when I started to feel pain? She heard him tell me at the beginning of every session to let him know when I felt the twinge of pain as he manipulated my arm so he could stop. The answer to her question is what taught me about true *feel*.

I never had to tell Bill when I felt the slightest twinge of pain because, like magic, just as he was approaching that point he would release the pressure ever so slightly. This caused me to relax. It was as if he could feel the pain even before I did. He knew the *feel* he was seeking. He knew what it felt like even better than I did. Because he could sense this *feel* his timing for the release was always perfect. His perfect timing of the release is what created the soft *feel*. The quick release resulted in me being even more relaxed and supple. I understood and trusted his touch. Therefore, I was more willing to let him move my arm a little further each time.

The thing which amazed me the most is Bill had better *feel* on me than I had on myself when I did the same exercises at home. I found I often pushed myself beyond the twinge of pain. The result was not only unpleasant it was less effective. As I pondered my lack of *feel* on myself, I wondered if I was doing the same thing to my horses.

I believe Bill had such good *feel* because he didn't have a rigid timeline set in his mind for when I needed to reach a particular goal. He was only interested in helping me achieve the maximum potential for excellent use of my arm again. In other words his skillful *feel* was married to the proper attitude. He was much more patient with me than I was with myself. I wanted to be done with the whole process yesterday. I learned when I became satisfied with slow and steady progress I began to relax making bigger strides than when I pushed myself too hard. I discovered by taking small steps it actually took less time.

As we endeavor to become good partners for our horses it is our responsibility to do what it takes to develop this kind of *feel* if we expect our horses to enjoy the relationship as much as we do. Because *feel* is all the horse has to go on! It is our job to figure out the whole horse, (his mind, body, and spirit). Then we must figure out what is missing on the inside of us which prevents us from finding the right *feel* for each individual horse. Finding *feel* may be a life long process. But each of us can find it with a strong desire to learn it, enough time, and someone to mentor us who's got more experience than we do working with horses through true *feel*. Anyone who learns true *feel* will get along better with horses. By consistent application of the principles in this book you can find a little piece of *feel* and therefore win your horse's heart!

Foreword

HORSE SENSE: Do You Have It?

"Animals are such agreeable friends - they ask no questions, they pass no criticisms." -- George Eliot

As I began writing this book I realized I couldn't explain how to win a horse's heart without first thinking back to how and why I adopted these ideas. I started thinking about how I became the horse lover I am today and about the principle I believe in. As I contemplated the transformation I comprehended it has been a very gradual and sometimes painful process starting at the tender age of two years old when my Dad bought me my first horse, named Ginger. I have been shaped by my family upbringing, environment, competition, education, faith in God, relationships, and the great horsemen and women I have aspired to learn from. The main influences and the reason for the change in my approach and attitude are the many horses I have had in my life. One particular horse which caused the most radical changes in me is a paint mare named Sunshine. I owe a lot of my growth and understanding to her. You'll hear more about Ginger and Sunshine later.

The ideas or principles presented in this book are not my own invention but rather are my own interpretation of what I have learned from others and experienced over forty years of both success and failure. Discovering my own mistakes has provided me with many of the correct answers to problems with horses and how to win their hearts. Although no one can know all the answers to every problem, the principles I offer in the pages of this book have been tested. I have experienced a high degree of success using these principles and so have the students I have helped. When these principles are applied with an attitude of confidence, compassion, and patience I have faith the recommendations I give here are good and true.

In order to win a horse's heart a common sense approach must be taken. I call this HORSE SENSE. But what is HORSE SENSE? Do horses have it? Are there any people who have it? Will HORSE SENSE elude us forever? Will some of us come to understand it in a way which helps us be safer, improve our relationship with horses, and have even more fun with our horses?

Some would call HORSE SENSE a knack, while others would say it's a skill. But for me, it is trying to figure out what makes horses and people tick. It has become my life's passion to discover and share ways people can find a common sense approach to horsemanship where ordinary people can get extraordinary results with their horses.

My early attempts at finding HORSE SENSE with my pony Ginger were without sophistication or any special knowledge. However, what I did have going for me was an unconscious awareness of how to be natural with horses. Maybe I did have a little of that inborn quality of *feel* necessary to winning a horse's heart. I also had sensitivity to what was right and wrong imparted to me by my parents. Ginger and I were partners in every way even though we lacked experience, training, and maturity. These are three of the basic ingredients which are vital to HORSE SENSE.

When I was old enough to compete in 4-H, rodeos, horse shows, and gymkhanas the partnership I had with horses seemed to change along with my ideas about HORSE SENSE. The pressure to win was both a good and bad influence on me. My judgment was sometimes clouded by my ultra ego to look and be the best. Therefore I often found myself doing things which were unfair and even unkind to my horse. As I look back I realize I lacked HORSE SENSE because I blamed my horse for my poor performance resulting in a loss. Then I took all the credit when I won.

I now see that temperance and refinement were two other qualities I still needed to develop in order to regain the partnership I had experienced with Ginger as a very young girl. On days when I would forget about my rigorous practice routine and just hang out with my horse by grooming, a free gallop in the pasture, or a swim in the river, I discovered a sense of balance which kept me on the path toward finding true HORSE SENSE.

The next leg of my journey for getting a taste of HORSE SENSE took me to the Howard Pitzer Ranch near Ericson, Nebraska. As I rode the colts assigned to me in the round pen, I kept my eyes glued on the other end of the arena where I watched Gary Putman, Howard's trainer at the time. My eyes were open to new ways as I watched with curiosity a reliable, savvy horseman with *feel*, timing and balance. His ability to decide with soundness what each horse needed was part of the refinement of HORSE SENSE I was still missing. I had a new conscious awareness that I had some raw talent, but I was a long way from being an artisan of horsemanship like I dreamed.

While working for a reining trainer in Montana for a very short time I met the first horse who scared me into paralyzing fear. I knew right away I didn't have the savvy to handle this situation. At least I was rational enough to get out of a very dangerous situation before I got hurt, due to my lack of knowledge, experience, and *feel*. I think this decision was using some HORSE SENSE.

Later another horse came into my life which left me puzzled, and frustrated. I found myself learning to put up with a lot of undesirable behavior as normal. In reality Slick was training me about what not to do when around him. It was the first horse I couldn't load in a trailer, put a bridle on over his ears, worm him, or give him shots. He was difficult to catch, trim his hooves, he spooked a lot and he pulled back when tied. Other than that he was the perfect horse. Of course, I loved him and so I learned to live with all of these problems. I tried to solve a couple of these problems through a local horse whisperer nick-named Pistol Pete. I begged him to show me how to put the bridle on over his sensitive ears and load him in the trailer. Pistol Pete accomplished these tasks in no time with ease because he had *feel*. But after he left I still couldn't do them.

After many years of success, a suit case full of buckles and ribbons, plus a wall full of trophies, I realized I had quite a bit of experience with horses, but no formal training, and I wasn't as smart as I thought I was. I had to admit what I understood about horses, why they do what they do, and how to handle each situation in a positive, progressive, and conscious manner was minimal at best.

Once I opened my mind to the fact I needed help if I was going to be one of those people with HORSE SENSE a whole new horse world appeared to me which I never knew existed. I became a learn-aholic, reading everything I could get my hands on. I went to as many clinics, camps, and lessons as I could afford. I watched videos over and over. I took notes on everything and kept diaries of my progress.

I spent hours and hours learning from horses. This was something new for me, because in the past my attitude and motivation were much different. Previous to this awakening I did things (to horses). I just saddled 'em up and rode. With a new understanding and purpose my intention changed to do things (with and for horses).

I am fortunate because I have been given many valuable opportunities to learn through   people who have asked me for lessons and entrusted me with their horses. It is both an honor and challenge to try to figure out how to communicate to another person how and why I am doing a particular thing with a horse. I have learned more than I ever thought possible through teaching others, because it causes me to think and focus on what I am doing and why. I want to be sure I am giving good solutions and correct information, so this causes me to research, and grow even more.

I'm sure I don't have absolute perfect HORSE SENSE yet. But I do know that experience, training, and maturity have taught me many of the pieces of the puzzle necessary to win a horse's heart. I may still be missing a couple pieces but the picture is coming into full view for me now. I know as I improve my understanding of what makes horses and people tick I will become the kind of horsewoman my horses need me to be in order to win their hearts and therefore get extraordinary results with them.

A person who has HORSE SENSE knows safety is always of the utmost importance when handling horses. Therefore the suggestions I give are based on utilizing the way the horse thinks and is capable of learning, acting, and moving. I believe in the old adage an ounce of prevention is better than a pound of cure.

We cannot over-emphasize thoughtfulness, a plan, and constant awareness of the handler in order to encourage the horse to do what we want before he does what we don't want. Being proactive instead of reactive is the foundational key of a safe approach to horsemanship. We cannot eliminate all risk involved with handling horses but we can reduce the risk by learning to be more proactive. This means using preventative practices which will help ensure our safety instead of cures which will take longer and cost more. It is good HORSE SENSE to use preventative medicine. We won't do ourselves or our horse any favors when we use quick fixes which are most of the time dangerous to both the horse and handler and often result in injury, either physical or mental.

A proactive horseman emphasizes awareness at all times of the environment, the horse, and their own mental, emotional, and physical fitness. Making a habit of staying alert in order to head off problems before they get out of hand is common HORSE SENSE.

A proactive approach can keep the horse from the notion of doing the wrong thing because the proper aids are given at the correct time, which results in the appropriate response. Then the response is reinforced with the kind of reward which is valuable to the horse. Bad habits can be prevented from developing using this approach. Being proactive means a constant attentiveness to keep a horse doing the right thing instead of waiting to correct mistakes after the fact, which is being reactive.

A reactive handler finds himself in situations where he is too often trying to win physical confrontations with the horse.

When this happens the horse can end up feeling wrong. With a reactive approach both the horse and the handler may get upset or even resentful. This happens because the reactive horseman has missed the opportunity to praise the horse for doing something well. The conversation sounds like this: "No, don't do that, or that, and that, not that either. Don't do this, nor that, and definitely not that." Instead of "Yes, that is what I asked." The worst part is when one waits too long to interrupt bad habits or make fair corrections the results is often a high risk situation for both the horse and the human. It makes good HORSE SENSE to do less sooner, instead of more later. Letting the problem grow and then trying to outmuscle the horse doesn't work no matter what kind of gadgetry we use. By being a proactive horseman who can recognize the early symptoms of a problem we can save ourselves and our horse a lot of misery.

When we find ourselves in an undesirable predicament with a horse it is tempting to put a band-aid on the trouble rather than cure it. A quick fix is anything that doesn't deal with the root of the problem or attempts to cover it up. In order to cure any horse problem one has to back up and retrain him the way it should have been done in the first place. Good HORSE SENSE is a matter of replacing bad habits with good ones for both the horse and the horse handler. This will take time and a considerable amount of effort.

The trouble is that retraining a horse and a person is four or five times harder than doing it right the first time. It isn't just a case of finding more ways of forcing or loving the horse into obedience. It is a case of retraining the handler so the horse can respond better.

If a horse does not respond the way the handler anticipated there is something incorrect with the way the person presented the request. Unless there are physical problems which prevent the horse from performing the desired task, something is causing the horse to be uncertain or unwilling. That something could be, and often is, the person on the end of the lead or in the saddle. If a horse is physically capable of doing what is asked, it is up to the practical horseman to ask in such a way that the horse will do it without resistance.

There is a solution to every problem. It is up to every horse owner to find solutions that work for each horse and situation. All of us will have more HORSE SENSE when we discover that most of the answers to our horse's problems are in finding our own mistakes. When we are able to do this we will find solutions that will work.

When a person has HORSE SENSE they have learned how to read every horse because they know that each horse is different. Every horse must be viewed as an absolute individual. A horseman with sound judgment also acknowledges that a horse can change in a moment depending on the time, situation, and circumstances. HORSE SENSE tells us that how well we are able to read a horse will determine what we can do with him. To be effective with horses we must be able to read them in the here and now and not limit them with labels.

A person who has HORSE SENSE puts emphasis on understanding the horse and responding to that understanding. A practical horseman realizes that every single thing which happens to a horse in the man-made environment we have put them in happens to them because we decided that it would. This realization imparts a compelling sense of responsibility. This responsibility renders a duty for horse lovers to become the most sensible and beneficial horseman they can be for their horse.

May you have more fun than you ever dreamed possible as you travel the road toward HORSE SENSE. May you ride safer and give your horse the best gift ever, a savvy partner with some HORSE SENSE. I believe your horse already has all the HORSE SENSE he needs. He's just waiting for you to catch up with him.

Sherry Jarvis

"However beautiful the strategy, you should occasionally look at the results." -- Sir Winston Churchill

Ginger and Sherry growing up together.

INTRODUCTION

"The road to success is always under construction."--
Anonymous

Letting Go and Being Open to Change

It is a near impossible task to teach all we need to know about
the horse/human relationship in one book. I don't presume I
can do it because I don't know all there is to know on this
subject. I would no longer be the kind of person who can
become a great horseman and win a horse's heart if I thought
I knew it all. However, I will do my best to share a way of
being with horses which works, no matter who you are or
what activity you choose to do with a horse.

Anyone who wants to win a horse's heart and learn to
ride a horse as a partner (as opposed to being a pilot who
micromanages, or a dictator who oppresses) will need to
set aside some old habits, patterns, and beliefs. We cannot
have it both ways. Many different philosophies cannot be
fit together and become harmonious horsemanship. We will
not get to where we want to be with a horse if we try to take
a little bit from one philosophy and stitch it together with a
little bit from another one. This can be discouraging news
to some people because it means they will have let go of
any habit, pattern, or belief which no longer fits into what
is best for the horse.

1

In addition to letting go of some ideas, the person will also need to be willing to make some personal changes. It doesn't mean we have to give up all we know and have worked so hard to learn through lessons, clinics, and the school of hard knocks. But many of the myths and ideas we have about riding and handling horses are going to have to die before we will be able to win a horse's heart. I have been around horses all of my life and it was a painful experience when I realized I knew very little correct information about the inner workings of a horse. I was always looking for what was wrong with the horse. It never crossed my mind I could have been the one who was wrong.

Part of learning is figuring out and admitting we don't know something. Until we come face to face with the fact that we may need to make some changes in the way we do things, growth will be minimal. It is impossible to teach anyone anything until they are ready for it. They have to be willing to open their mind and start over if that is what it takes. For many people they aren't ready to do this until they hit rock bottom with a horse. Even though these people are about to throw in the towel by getting rid of the horse, there is still something inside them which says "I don't want to give up". Failure or injury with a horse is often what it takes to get a person ready and willing to discover more about what it takes to succeed and be safe with horses. However, there are other horsemen who innately want to take their relationship with their horse to the next step. These people like to learn and can't seem to get enough. No matter what category you fall into, learning can be fun and rewarding even with the difficulties involved.

The first step in altering our point of view about horse training is to start looking at and consider things from the horse's point of view. We have the mental capacity to do this, but a horse cannot do the same. Only when we begin to think like a horse will we be able to outsmart any horse. In order to get an honest response back from a horse we must first convey clarity to the horse. Training a horse takes a good deal of honesty, openness, insight, observation, thinking, problem solving, common sense, and humor.

This is not a "how to book" of horse training techniques; rather it is about becoming the kind of horseman who can win any horse's heart. We've all seen the person who can walk in a pen with a horse and make an instant connection. What makes this person different from everyone else? Are they born with this talent or is it learned? I believe it is a little bit of both. But what sets the great horseman apart from the average one is the ability to establish a rapport with the horse and maintain it through consistent fair leadership and *feel* that is meaningful to the horse. The type of leadership and *feel,* or the lack thereof, we are able to offer a horse will make the difference between success and failure of winning his heart.

The term leadership as I will use it throughout this book is not synonymous with boss. It is not about the human gaining a sense of power or superiority over the horse. It is more about developing a working relationship through teaching and leadership.

Before I go any further I think it is important to define leadership and teacher. In the dictionary leadership is said to be the capacity to lead, or the position of a leader. A leader is a person who has authority or influences. A leader provides supervision, gives direction, assistance, and support as needed. A good teacher also does these things. A teacher is someone who imparts information or skills so that others may learn with a specific end in view. Teaching also implies

the development of the mind. A teacher facilitates proper
training, which develops appropriate habits. Correct habits
offer an advantage towards success in any endeavor.

In addition to providing leadership and *feel* for a horse, a
high-quality horseman is also the horse's teacher. Many times
I have found there is a role reversal and the horse becomes
the teacher. Every humble horseman who wants to win a
horse's heart is open to letting the horse teach him. In the end
it is every horseman's job to educate a horse so that he can
understand and accept whatever we ask him to do and be all
right with it. The horse needs to be ok with it on the inside
not just on the outside. Through education we can help the
horse accept with confidence whatever situation we ask him
to be in. When we have accomplished this we have reached
an exceptional kind of HORSE SENSE.

Carrots or Whips?

There is a distinct pecking order in a herd of horses. This
pecking order is an important element of horse relationships.
There seem to be two schools of thought on this subject when
it comes to injecting the human into these relationships. One
says we have to dominate the horse through force, fear, and
intimidation. On the other side some think they can win a
horse's heart with kindness and cookies alone. Insufficient
firmness with a horse confuses him just as much as bullying.
Neither of these horse handlers can provide the clear leadership
or teaching every horse needs. These two types of horse
handlers are on opposite swings of the same pendulum. The
truth lies somewhere in the middle with a balanced approach
based on patience, compassion, and a longing to understand
the horse. When the horse is finally understood, a desire is
often born within a sensitive horseman to become a useful
leader and functional teacher. A leader/teacher is an insightful

horseman who rewards the slightest try, then is also willing to use assertiveness and correction in the proper amount when needed. Notice I didn't use the term punishment. Horses do not understand the concept of punishment.

If we watch with care the pattern in horse behavior, we will see when one horse gets ready to grab some food, there is an immediate reaction from another horse, like a kick or bite. The bite or kick comes *before* the first horse grabs the food. On the other hand, punishment is done *after* the infraction, which is too late for behavior modification. Plus, punishment is often administered with anger which is out of control and vengeful, not to mention that there is no educational value in punishment. Effective leaders are tuned in enough to ward off or divert undesirable behavior. They use positive reinforcement which builds respect and trust instead of punishment which can build resentment and disrespect.

Winning a horse's heart is not about carrots and worrying about whether the horse will like you or not, any more than it is about being a rough and tough boss. It is about being clear. In order to be clear to a horse we need to understand how he thinks, what drives his actions, and how he responds and communicates with other horses. We need to think, act, play, and speak like a horse. When we do this we become far better equipped to control the horse in a way which is not only clear to the horse but safer for us. It is safer because if we know what a horse is going to do before he does it, we can prevent it.

The term "dominance" implies a social hierarchy, not an abusive dictatorship. There is a difference in this social hierarchy depending on the amount of physical area allocated to the herd. For example horses in the wild may not have as many reasons to defend their personal space as much as corralled horses. Clashes within the herd over survival necessities such as food and water may not be as common or violent when sufficiency is available. The driving force behind territorial disputes depends on many factors which I don't have time or space to discuss in depth here. However, we can state the obvious. The smaller the quarters in which horses are kept, the more they seem to have to protect their space. Crowded conditions seem to increase the amount of confrontations. As a result of these facts, horse behavior may vary depending on the conditions in which we place them. Since most of us don't interact with horses in their natural habitat I will focus on what I have observed from horses that have become domesticated. My experience with feral horses is very limited. I have spent a little time in Nevada and Wyoming watching some wild herds but not enough to deem myself an expert by any means.

If we observe the hierarchy of a horse herd in the human environment we have placed them in, we discover the alpha horse has a position of authority with controlling influence over certain necessities like, food, water, shelter etc. They do this by moving their subordinates around with body language which communicates, "I have a margin over you." They start with a look but will resort to hooves and teeth when needed. There is often a great deal more noise and bluffing than actual violence. Although the dominant horse has a superior social position the purpose behind their commanding rule seems to be the protection, safety and peace of the herd. Once the order is established the lower ranking horses follow the higher ones and challenges are less frequent. When everyone understands their place in the hierarchy there is order within the herd which provides security.

We also fit into the pecking order of the herd. Once a horse accepts our higher position, they will follow us and even begin to rely on us. However, we cannot establish ourselves in the equine order by force or by being a door mat; instead we must do it in the same manner as a horse. A horse is a prey animal who dominates another horse by moving him out of his personal space, which is the exact opposite of the predator instinct of a human to dominate through immobilization. In order to be an effective leader for a horse we must reprogram our way of thinking and follow the example set by a lead horse.

If we provoke a fight we will always be on the losing end no matter how small the horse is. So we must use our superior brain rather than our inferior strength. Our leadership must project calm authority and confidence. Horses read and understand leadership just as well as they can detect fear and uncertainty. We exert our authority by moving the horse and setting boundaries, not by trapping and immobilizing him. By guiding and directing the movements and activities of a horse we are establishing a precedent of rank. This type of leadership is not an unrestrained or tyrannical exercise of power determined by the leader's preference or convenience, rather it is a reasonable act of compassion out of necessity for the preservation of the herd.

For a horse to have faith in our leadership he needs to believe that we will take care of him and that we are always present and aware of issues that are a concern to him. Our field of awareness needs to include the horse's sphere of awareness. The horse needs to know that we perceive the things he perceives. When we notice what the horse notices he can trust us and thus feel safe. An attentive leader is not less aware of the environment than the horse. A conscientious horseman with calm authority will not push a horse through thresholds just to get him to perform a certain task.

To illustrate this, I was riding one of my horses on a very familiar trail. As we popped up over a hill there was a tractor tire lying in a blowout (a term we use in the sandhills for a sand dune). We had ridden by this spot many times before, but never from this side or angle. My horse stopped instantly snorting with her nostrils flared and her eyes bulging in fear. I could feel her feet wanting to gallop off without restraint. My first reaction was a moment of stillness in which I called on those qualities of calm leadership that would help both of us. In that moment of stillness I was thinking, "Courage, resolve, trust and confidence. Don't make a big deal out of this. Remember to BREATHE."

Instead of dashing off in fear or spinning out of control as she had done in the past when our relationship was weaker. My horse began stretching her neck out in order to better examine the horse-eating tractor tire about to pounce out of the sand. Then she leaned forward with curiosity and her feet began to move carefully. Thirty seconds later we were walking down the hill in the deep sand by the tractor tire with peaceful resolve. The encompassing power of a moment of calm, confident stillness where we clarify our intention, and affirm positive outcomes is a strategy I consciously use often with horses. It's effectiveness to influence a horse in many situations is astonishing.

On the flip side, unrestrained use of power can turn into illogical punishment. I have watched riders giving their horse a smack with a whip or a jab with a spur because he refused to cross water, go through a gate, inside a roping box, over a jump, around a barrel, or many other requests. In fact I have also reacted this way in an act of desperation. A rider can justify these actions all day long, saying the horse was being naughty by refusing and they were just teaching him a lesson. However, I don't think the horse really knows that his refusal was the reason for the punishment or that he should never refuse again in order to avoid future punishment.

Horses have reasons for doing what they do. In their world those reasons are perfectly valid. The truth may be the horse refused because he was afraid or unsure whether he could perform the command. When these kinds of things happen the horse is usually trying to tell us that all is not well with some aspect of his world. He could also be saying he is sick and tired of something. Before we ever resort to punishment we should always try to find the cause of the undesirable behavior because if we continue punishing him he may stop trying to tell us. When this happens the situation will become so intolerable for the horse that he can become dangerous due to his extreme anxiety. At this point if we punish him for being dangerous someone is bound to get hurt and we shouldn't blame the horse for the injuries.

Language and Lifestyle

If you are new to the horse world you have discovered we have our own language. This language and the terms we use change by geographical region and also according to the discipline we choose. It boils down to this: No matter what language we use, good horsemanship is effective communication through *feel*. We also have a lot of catch phrases. As I repeat these expressions I am not assigning them to any one person because we have been repeating them for so long I'm not sure anyone knows who first said them. One of the idioms I hear over and over from respectable horsemen is *"Make the wrong thing difficult, and the right thing easy. But put the emphasis on making the right thing easy."* Making the right thing easy takes more thinking and insight, and foresight and planning, than making the wrong thing difficult. This may include thinking about how to present a release for the horse to move into rather than a pressure to move away from. If we can make this our lifestyle, a horse will not only become a reliable companion, but we will win his heart.

A good leader realizes horsemanship is a journey more than a destination. It is a lifestyle and in order to live this way sometimes we will:

- Be the leader or we may be led
- Be the teacher or the student
- Forgive or need to be forgiven
- Have fears or be brave
- Progress well or endure plateaus
- Succeed or fail
- Rejoice or shed a few tears
- Have clarity or be confused
- Rush or slow down to take the time it takes
- Feel like we have arrived at a destination or like we may never get there.

But most of all an effective leader or teacher will keep an open mind and allow freedom to experiment. If we do this, our journey will take us to destinations beyond our original intention.

Principles: Enrich Life and Ensure Success

The purpose of this book is to motivate and inspire horse lovers toward a life style which leads to excellence with horses where we develop the habit of going above and beyond what is accepted as normal. When certain principles are followed our success will be ensured. These principles are the primary focus of this book. Each chapter will discuss two terms or concepts which may be opposed to one another or perhaps at times may work to compliment each another. Every instructional chapter is followed by a true personal story demonstrating successful application of the principles.

The reason I have chosen to focus on principles rather than technique is that even the best techniques can fail, or worse yet, can cause physical or emotional damage to the horse when applied with unscrupulous principles. Two different people can use the same technique and get very different results depending on the principles they use to apply the technique. A principle is the habitual development of a code of conduct. Every principle we have has an underlying faculty of human nature such as greed or curiosity. The quality of character which we exhibit is determined by the faculties we base our principles upon. The result we get with any appropriate technique is determined by our principles.

The other reason I am not explaining training techniques and the step by step process to get your horse to do a certain task is because there are plenty of good books and tapes already published on this. It doesn't matter what discipline you choose with a horse there is a program available which can help you learn the necessary techniques. I encourage every horse owner to buy an appropriate program and educate themselves on techniques. Although reading about them in a book is helpful, it alone is not the most effective way for most people to learn good technique. Without hands-on experience, instruction, and watching horsemen who already excel in the technique, a person is often left disappointed or worse yet, confused.

By reading the principles contained throughout this book I expect to challenge your thinking. I will provide stimulating questions which may guide you to discovery about yourself, your horsemanship philosophy, techniques, and goals. As you read and think I ask you to re-examine and hone your beliefs, allowing yourself permission to make adjustments when necessary. Let the ideas presented enrich your life even if you don't agree with every one of them. I hope by reading the principles and concepts contained within the pages of this book you will become an even better horseman so you can win your horse's heart and live your horse dreams to the fullest.

As you develop these horsemanship principles you will discover they will also apply to other areas of your life. I have noticed many of the principles used to develop a relationship with a horse and improve our performance also work with other relationships. If you learn to win a horse's heart you may be surprised you will also have the wherewithal to win the hearts of many. When we win someone's heart we can become a positive influence and therefore make a difference in the world one heart at a time.

Chapter 1: Natural vs. Normal

"A true horseman does not look at the horse with his eyes; he looks at his horse with his heart." ~Author Unknown

The Unexplainable Attraction to Horses

I believe man and horse have a special bond. There is almost a mystical quality as if we were made to be together. The horse seems to be the only prey animal we have this strong desire to bond with. Not many of us obsess about wanting to ride other prey animals like: cows, deer, elk, etc. The draw of the horse is a powerful force which can cause obsession in a person so deep they are willing to risk life and limb in order to live a dream.

Many humans are driven to know the horse, to make friends with it, to teach it, and to learn from it. But more than anything else we seem to want to harness its freedom, power, and beauty. I often wonder how and when this relationship first began. From what I have read there is a very long history filled with brutality as well as miraculous and inspiring stories between horses and mankind.

One thing which inspires and draws us to this wondrous creature is the horse's adaptability. The reason horses have survived millions of years of abuse, conflict, and friendship with us is their ability to make incredible constant changes. It is just short of a miracle that a cautious, claustrophobic,

coward who is also a panic-aholic can trust the ultimate
predator on earth to the point where a harmonious ride is
achieved.

Those of us who love horses believe they are nature in its
finest form. We are humbled by the fact that an animal so in
tune with nature would be willing to accept us as a partner.
Having a relationship with a horse is to feel close to nature.
There is an unexplainable natural attraction and affection
in a horse lover which is flamed by respect and passion to
protect the spirit, dignity, and curiosity of the horse. The
excellent horsemanship we can see being displayed today
was ignited by this flame centuries ago. It is nothing new.
Because of the accessibility of the mass media the flame
is burning even brighter now. There are no new training
techniques or principles for us to learn because the ones
being taught are very old.

This is an exciting time to be learning about horsemanship
because if a person is serious about becoming an excellent
horseman there are countless opportunities. There are a
large number of people with very diverse backgrounds and
levels of experience that have a growing passion to learn true
horsemanship through *feel*. Every day I am seeing more and
more people who are interested in becoming worthy human
partners for their horses. However there seems to be some
debate among horse people about what true horsemanship
through *feel* is. Some use the term "natural horsemanship"
in order to describe a way of life with horses. Others are
offended by classification of horsemanship using the word
"natural" saying this is just a fad. Some of the debate may be
due to semantics or because of a lack of direct experience or
deep contemplation.

Through my own extensive research, experience, and

thoughtful consideration I am going to attempt to identify what may be implied by the obscure term "natural horsemanship". My aim is NOT to defend or justify any position, nor is it to judge any person, their techniques, values, or viewpoints. Rather I wish to unite horse lovers toward improved quality of life for both horses and their partners.

Most misconceptions are cultivated when a person doesn't understand what is involved if they base their opinion on hearsay and prejudices rather than on personal study and experience. When a person has never experienced anything different, or is afraid to try something new, then it is understandable that they may be confused. These misunderstandings have caused the controversy of natural vs. normal. Or maybe we could say:

- knowledge and skills vs common habits
- unexpected partnership vs typical routine
- instinctual interactions vs conventional training

The term "natural horsemanship" is nothing more than an inadequate label for a "way of life with horses". This approach to horsemanship is based upon common sense, positive outcomes, and appropriate attitudes. It is difficult to put a "way of life" into words. It is easier to see a "way of life" put into action where a pleasant and successful relationship is the product of living sensible principles.

I have heard the argument that there is nothing natural about horsemanship. Some people believe it is impossible to do anything natural with horses because any time we intermingle with a horse it is not natural for the horse. If this is true then I guess the only natural thing for us to do is turn them all out into the wild and no longer have interactions with them. This may be the ultimate definition of what is natural for the horse. I can't argue with this. But the fact still remains that millions of people do relate with horses every day. So we need to figure out a way which is most natural and palatable for the horse.

There are hundreds of different ways humans have proposed as the right or only way to relate with horses. It is quite possible that none of these ways are what Mother Nature planned. But I can't help but wonder: Can we presume this? Was it in the mind of the creator for us to interact with horses from the beginning? Perhaps he knew this relationship could teach us a few things about nature and character? What about the natural curiosity of the horse? Is it possible the horse offered this relationship to us first? Who can determine whether the horse was intended to be a part of us or not?

Define True Horsemanship

By defining what "natural" is we can attempt to clear up some of the confusion and controversy about what the term "natural horsemanship" implies?

Webster's dictionary describes "natural" as:
- Being in accordance with or determined by nature based on an inherent sense of right and wrong or justice
- Having an essential relation with someone or something
- An inborn talent occurring in conformity with the ordinary course of nature
- Possessing or exhibiting the higher qualities of human nature like kindness and affection
- Marked by easy simplicity and freedom from artificiality or constraint
- Without pretense

- Having a spontaneousness
- Something that is likely to become an immediate success

Horsemanship according to Webster's is "a rider or driver of horses; one whose skill in caring for or managing horses is exceptional.

By putting the two terms "natural" and "horsemanship" together an identity is produced which needs further explanation in order to describe a philosophical and practical life style with horses.

Based upon the above definitions, "natural horsemanship" is people reaching toward exceptional skill in caring for and managing horses in accordance with the nature of the horse. This is achieved by developing an essential relationship based on justice, kindness, and affection without the use of artificial constraints. Both the person and horse are free to be spontaneous with creative expressions. There is a marked, easy simplicity in the approach used to develop harmony without pretense. Success is guaranteed when curiosity, dignity, and spirit are preserved by remaining true to the inborn characteristics and talent of both the horse and the human.

Through my research and experience natural horsemanship is an approach to learning. In this approach we must move out of our comfort zone with a willingness to experiment, think and make mistakes. Slowing down and remaining flexible when things go wrong is also necessary. But one of the most important attitudes we must be able to leave behind is negative judgment of the horse. We must not focus on his previous owners or any bad experiences we think may have caused his undesirable behaviors.

The statement, "natural horsemanship is an approach to learning," causes us to evaluate ourselves with honesty. By examining our approach to horsemanship we discover our greatest challenge often lies in mastering our own thoughts, emotions, and physical inadequacies before learning to control a horse. When we have gained a thorough understanding of the horse and become proficient enough to master our own thoughts, emotions, and physical limitations a new conscious awareness is available to us. It is through this conscious awareness we are able to distinguish how a horse perceives us and what he needs from us. When we are able to grasp things from the horse's viewpoint we can respond to his natural condition with more clarity. A conscious awareness and dedication to clarity is what being natural with a horse is about. This is what sets the distinguished horsemen apart from the ordinary.

That Horse Has Heart! Becoming Extraordinary

A natural approach to horsemanship doesn't include quick fixes which give us instant success and self gratification. Rather it is a self improvement program where we win something much more valuable than a ribbon, trophy, buckle or money. Success and satisfaction are found in winning a horse's heart! When a person declares "that horse has heart," he has not only recognized an inborn quality, but he knows the horse has been given the opportunity to share and develop this gift in an environment where trust and respect resulted in a willing exuberance to perform.

Once a horse's heart is won, the things a person can accomplish with him are no longer mediocre, but a limitless potential exists where dreams come true. However in order to reach this level of excellence one must be dedicated to changing

with the horse. It will be necessary to quit blaming the horse
for problems and start mastering our own thoughts, emotions
and physical inadequacies.

Through a natural approach to horsemanship many people
have been able to progress way beyond what most people
think horses and humans are capable of doing together. Every
day people have achieved things with certain troubled horses
which many critics thought was impossible. Opportunities
for success abound when we open our eyes to the possibilities
and are willing to do what it takes.

In the process of learning and applying the principles and
skills of horsemanship in a natural way, other areas of life
are affected, causing a powerful metamorphosis of the
person. Things which used to unsettle us are now no big
deal. Creativity, confidence, communication, leadership, and
problem solving skills improve. Attitudes towards horses and
life in general will change so much it will be reflected in our
personal and business life. When this happens, both people
and horses will notice and wonder what happened to us.

The Principles Behind the Techniques

Is this natural way of cooperating and understanding horses
for everyone? In a perfect world the answer is yes, because
I know the tremendous benefits. But in the real world some
will choose another path. For lack of a better term we will
refer to any other path as "normal". This means any approach
which doesn't stay true to principles that by their moral fiber
put the true nature of the horse in the forefront are not natural.
This doesn't mean a "normal" way is ineffective or wrong.
However, some of the common practices which are accepted
in a "normal" world are not always in the best interest of the
horse because they do not preserve his spirit, dignity, trust,

or curiosity. There are some things which are not negotiable. Whenever a practice borders on cruelty where the mental, emotional, and physical state of the horse is compromised for the sake of human goals, it should not be tolerated by anyone who claims to love horses. We should always ask these questions: How does the horse feel? Do our techniques, principles, and goals improve life for the horse, or not?

Many of the same techniques are used by people who claim to be a "natural horseman" and those who do not. There are some people who are very "natural" with horses even if they don't label themselves as such. The main difference between the horseman who is natural with horses and one who is not is the principles behind their techniques.

Remember a principle is a habitual code of conduct. I am sure the following list of principles, which every fine horseman aspires to, is incomplete because I am still learning. As a matter of fact, that is the first and most important principle. Are you still learning? Or, do you think you know it all? All first-class horsemen remain in a learning frame of mind with an attitude of humility and a desire for growth as long as they are on the journey. Here are some other codes of conduct which become habitual to the unpretentious horseman. Many of these principles will be discussed in further detail later in the book.

1. Work on self first.
2. Believe in your horse; trust him
3. Confidence, curiosity, and dignity of the horse are priorities
4. Trust and respect in equal amounts. The goal is to preserve the horse's spirit
5. Think; have a plan and still allow for creativity
6. Every moment counts. Everything means something, so observe & compare

7. Prepare for everything. A proper foundation leads to success
8. Present tasks with a purpose in mind, but remain flexible and don't drill
9. Consistency and variety are both necessary, depending on the situation
10. Direct and then support
11. Always do as little as it takes, but be willing to do what it takes
12. Learn to be assertive and keep aggression at bay.
13. Take the time it takes. With patience & compassion it will take less time.
14. Offer meaningful soak time for the horse to absorb learning. This will improve retention.
15. Use positive reinforcement by rewarding the slightest try
16. Pressure is motivation to find the right thing.
17. Release is the reward for finding the right thing
18. The approach is important but the retreat is even more critical
19. Know when to quit
20. Put these principles before lofty goals and you will win a horse's heart.

A Turning Point

Most people who have horses love them and want what's best for them. There are some who have found a special relationship with a horse which is rewarding for both the human and the horse. Others are still seeking and desiring this, while some don't even know it exits. Then there is a small group of sour apples whose motivations are questionable. Some of these people will do just about anything to win a competition whether it is what is best for the horse or not. I know. I have been there.

Those of us who may claim to be "natural" are not better human beings than those who don't follow the same principles. The thing we must look at is the relationship. If the relationship is a mess it doesn't matter whether the person claims to be "natural" or not, or how many awards they have won. What matters most is the relationship.

Everyone is at a different place on this journey. As long as a person has an open mind with a willingness to listen and try new things they will continue to progress in a positive natural way. It doesn't mean we no longer make mistakes. The critical difference lies in the fact we learn from each mistake. If we can learn from other people's mistakes without judging them, then we have made substantial progress as a true learner. There is always value in our effort to try to be the best we can and learn as much as possible even if we haven't arrived yet. However, it is time for concern when a person believes they have arrived with nothing more to learn.

Most successful people have a turning point in their life. Mine was when I made a clear specific, unequivocal decision to not go on with horses as I had been. When I went to my first horsemanship clinic I saw right away what I had been missing. I knew I needed to change. From the moment I saw people interacting with their horses in a different way than I was accustomed to I knew then and there my life with horses would never be the same. I knew beyond a shadow of a doubt I was going to succeed with horses better than I ever had in the past. Some people have this turning point at a very early age, others have it much later in life, and then there are a few who never make the decision to look beyond where they are.

I believe there is also a turning point in every horse's life. Even though every horse has inborn characteristics, there is a defining moment in their life which has a great influence on how they will relate with humans until they die. This one instance or experience may be good or bad. It may not appear to humans as any big deal, but to the horse it is. If we do not believe everything we do with a horse matters, or if we are not paying attention we may miss this significant moment.

These defining moments are not limited to a single one. There are usually a series of turning points. Those who remain in a diligent state of awareness will be able to take advantage of these opportunities which can turn an average horse into a great one in a twinkling of an eye. Horsemen who have an eye for these openings are the ones who can help a problem horse become an outstanding partner. These discerning horsemen are the ones who can win most any horse's heart because they not only recognize these moments but can even create them. I remember an emotional turning point for a little sorrel mare named Lexie, with a flaxen mane and tail. She belonged to a woman who is seeking more HORSE SENSE! It was about Sharon's third clinic with me. I asked her permission to see if we could get Lexie to connect with a human. Because in all honesty I don't think she had ever truly connected with a person. Sharon said okay even though she admitted she didn't know what I meant. Some people think they have a decent connection with their horse but once in a while an opportunity appears where we find out there is more.

After roping off half of the large arena we removed her halter letting Lexie move freely. Then I played a little join up game with her where I mirrored her moves. Every time Lexie even gazed in my direction I walked the other way. This relieved all pressure on her, impressing upon her that I was not trying to get her to do anything. It wasn't long before Lexie was following me everywhere at liberty in the big arena. Up until this time she had a nasty hard glint in her eye. Now her eyes were soft and accepting.

I then asked Sharon if she would like to try it. She said she prayed to God that her horse would show her the same acceptance as quickly as she had shown it to me. It did take a little longer. Sharon said this made her sad because she took it as a personal condemnation from her horse. She was thinking her horse didn't love her even though she always takes such good care of her. Sharon said this was very hard for her to swallow. But later she discovered it wasn't personal. It was just her horse being a horse in the best way she knew how given the environmental experiences and innate characteristics that belong to her.

With encouragement from her friend Leigh and on my prompting Sharon kept trying to   do what I instructed her to do. As she recalls the experience these are the things she heard and thought: Okay, now don't look at her. Quick walk away from her! Relax and breathe! WHAT? All right! I'll just do what you say even though I don't really understand how this works or why. I will trust the process anyway.

Sharon says it seemed like forever before Lexie finally made the decision to be with her. She remembers she broke down in tears when her horse came up to her standing humbly before her. She said she cried because the honor was so great. The rest of us had blurry eyes as well. It was a moment worth remembering.

That day was a breakthrough for both of them. After that point things took a turn for the better. From that day forward Sharon has endeavored to be with Lexie in a way that is best for her. She tries to understand Lexie's horseonality and read her properly. Because of that defining moment things have changed in their relationship. Sharon strives to keep the relationship happy and respectful. She is careful about doing things in ways which make sense to Lexie. That turning point keeps her ever mindful of what it takes for Lexie to give herself to a human. She says she doesn't ever want to make Lexie regret the decision she made that day to truly connect with a human. It was one of the greatest moments of Sharon's life and it was certainly a turning point for a little sorrel mare with a flaxen mane and tail. Since that day their progress together has been nothing short of amazing.

Have you made a clear specific unequivocal decision to take a more natural approach to horsemanship with a commitment to learn everything within your capabilities? Do you want to become exceptional with horses and win their hearts? Do you want to see things better from the horse's point of view? Nobody is going to do the work for you. In order to succeed it will take sweat, time, money and quite a few horses as your teachers before this approach becomes natural to you. You will have to make some sacrifices and go through uncomfortable changes, but the end result will be more than worth it when you can say, "my horse has heart!"

Ginger and Sherry at the Girl Scout Pet Show

GINGER: Kids are Naturally Natural; a Good Pony is Good for the Soul

Sherry and Ginger friends forever.

Grandma said she was the color of ginger spice, thus we named her Ginger. This exceptional Shetland pony would win the hearts of many for over thirty years. She was only two years old with big soft brown eyes, a white blaze on her face, and a long shaggy golden mane and tail when my dad bought her in 1960. He hand picked her for us because he wanted to share the love and passion he had for horses with his family, in hopes we would follow in his footsteps. I fell in love with Ginger from the moment I set eyes on her, and I inherited my Dad's passion. Ginger was sent to school for a couple of years before I could ride her by myself since I was only two years old at the time dad bought her.

Ginger went to live with my uncle Dale on an isolated ranch in the sandhills of central Nebraska. He had three boys older than me who rode her several miles to school every day. These boys were rough tough cowboys. I am pretty sure they didn't have much finesse when it came to horse training. But because they were fearless and since she was their transportation to school they got the job done. When Ginger came back home Dad says at first he led me from the ground while I rode. It wasn't long and he was leading me from the back of his rope horse Jobe. He laughs when he remembers how tight I held on to the saddle horn when he asked if I was ready to trot. I guess he almost needed a pry bar to get me off that pony. I remember one time I rode so long I peed my pants because I didn't want to get off Ginger.

And so began a life long relationship with a special pony that was easy to get along with. Not the typical reputation of a Shetland pony. If she had any bad behaviors I don't remember them. My Mom says she didn't like baths but I don't remember this. Instead I recall she rather liked water, because I used to swim in the river with her. I try to recall frustrations or disagreements with Ginger but all I can see in my memory is fun, love and a friend who never let me down. Everyone who met Ginger loved and adored her.

I think the reason I didn't have difficulties with Ginger was because I was natural with her. Kids can do this because they don't analyze everything which can end up making the simple things complicated. I didn't know how to do anything except be myself with her and enjoy each moment. I was able to stay open, alert, and honest with myself and with her. This is the basis of being natural with a horse.

Being natural with a horse brings one closer to nature. There is an appreciation for nature inside a horse which causes the person who is around them to feel happy and even more alive. A good pony is just plain joy to the soul. There is a healing power the moment a connection is made between a horse and a person because the horse makes no judgments and his feedback is always honest.

The only time Ginger ever hurt anyone was when my brother fell off her and broke his arm. But it wasn't Ginger's fault. We were playing cowboys and Indians. The attack was on my brother. We were throwing dirt clods at him. Ginger was running from the dirt bullets being shot at her. She was running very fast and she could run. In fact we used to beat the big horses in the barrel racing with her at the local 4-H horse shows. Anyway, Steve was quite little, not more than five years old. When Ginger dodged a flying dirt clod he lost his balance and while trying to catch himself he snapped his arm. Of course, Ginger ran back to the barn without him. After he got back from the hospital we kept what happened that day a secret from our parents until we were in high school.

All my cousins, neighbors, and friends learned to ride on Ginger and years later even my nieces and nephews. My cousin Bruce even heeled steers on her. She put up with all of us in a patient way and even seemed to enjoy her jobs. One of her jobs was counselor. After I had gone off to college my Mom used to let the younger cousins ride her. She led them down the old railroad tracks near our place where the trains hadn't run in years. The relaxing ride on our friend Ginger caused the kids to share their secrets with her. Mom said she found out the latest scoop about all the relatives each time a child rode Ginger. She never told their secrets to anyone because it was as if they were sharing their soul with a friend they knew would never judge them. Horses are like that, they can reveal to us the truths about ourselves but while doing it they never judge us.

As a child I cried many a tear into Ginger's mane with the pains of growing up. I shared my secrets, hopes, and dreams with her as I rode along the meadows of the winding Loup River. Galloping Ginger with her mane and tail blowing in the wind made my imagination run wild. I was a rodeo queen, a jockey, a circus performer, a barrel racer at the NFR, and a show jumper in the Olympics as I cleared the bales of alfalfa hay in the field.

There wasn't anything we couldn't do or any place we couldn't go when we were together because of the natural relationship we had and the dreams of a little girl who loved her horse. When a horse becomes a part of you there are no limits to what you can do together. As an adult if I find myself getting frustrated with a horse or don't know what to do I think back to my simple relationship with Ginger. This gives me a fresh perspective where simple solutions based on honesty, humility, respect, and trust are always the answer.

Wait, I want to ride too! My little sister Jill
running to catch up with Dad &me.

There are no secrets to horse training. Contrary to our adult beliefs and ego, true horsemanship with *feel* is not re-invented by how smart we are, rather we re-discover it when we humble ourselves and let our minds become creative again. Kids are so natural with horses because they allow the process to happen by using clear imaginative thinking. They also choose to enjoy each moment of the journey. Being natural with a horse is a mixture of intuition, sensitivity, compassion, honesty, realism, experience, and fast thinking. There are innumerable ways to train a horse but it all still boils down to universal principles which are mandated by the horse's unique and constant nature. When it stops being about us and it starts being about the horse, his nature, and the relationship, we are on our way to being natural with a horse like we were when we were kids.

As adults we often forget that what the horse finds understandable, acceptable, and pleasurable, both physically and emotionally, is very different from what humans need. Poor training techniques fail because they ignore equine reality. A bad method cannot produce a truly good result. Good methods produce results because they are clear, visible, and useful to the mind of the horse and his reality. One person may get phenomenal results with a horse but this great outcome may not transfer when another person puts his foot in the stirrup. Good training for a horse won't hold if the person doesn't have access to it. The horse still has it but each person who interacts with him must know how to open it and then retrieve it.

A person who can relate to a horse the way a horse relates to another horse will get immediate lifelong compliance from the horse. The more simple, reasonable, and unmistakable the request, the better we will be able to relate to the horse.

The better we relate to the horse the better the relationship will be and therefore we will win our horse's heart.

Ginger captured my heart from the moment I laid eyes on her. The connection we had was real. I believe even though my techniques and skills were unsophisticated, as the years went by I won the heart of Ginger because I was natural with her and didn't know how to be anything else.

Dad holding Ginger while Sherry and
sister Jill ride together.

Chapter 2: Reality vs. Dreams

"Always bear in mind that your own resolution to succeed is more important than any one thing." -- Abraham Lincoln

Living in the Reality of the Moment

As discussed in the previous chapter, the first step toward winning a horse's heart is in developing an approach to horsemanship based on patience and compassion. The second secret of winning a horse's heart is living in the reality of the moment. We all have hopes and dreams of what we would like to accomplish or perfect with our horse one day. By being too concerned about the promise of a future we hope to achieve we often miss the fullness of the moment we could have experienced right here and now with a horse. I guarantee a horse hasn't given one single thought to these future dreams, because a horse lives in the moment. I think some horses learn to endure our tactics with patience but others show their agitation and we call them naughty or moody. Every single moment we are in the presence of a horse we are influencing them in either a positive or negative way. Yes, everything we do matters, even the little stuff.

A natural approach emphasizes how important the little things are. Most of the time we tend to focus on the big things like collection, sliding stops, lead changes, bits and tools, etc. because they are so often a big part of our dreams. Many of the problems and flaws in our performance can be traced back to something very simple. A small hole in our foundation can cause big problems, thus we need to keep the basics going even while advancing.

The reason that everything matters, even the little things, is because horses are PEOPLE EXPERTS! If we miss the small stuff it will turn into big stuff. Horses know what we know and more important they know what we don't know. We should never forget what a horse needs us to know. Isn't it amazing horses can and do most often figure out what we want even if we don't know what we should? I think this is because of who they are, not because of who we are, or how skilled we are.

A horse will come to our level of competence or incompetence. Our presence should bring out the best in a horse, not the worst. If our presence makes a horse upset we must make the necessary change in us which will make a difference for the horse. Don't expect the horse to change first because he is just living, surviving, and responding to the moment the best he knows how. His reality of that moment may not be the same as ours.

There are many ways a person's presence can upset a horse. It is obvious when a person is being exceedingly violent with a horse, causing him to explode in panic-stricken chaos, that the horse is disturbed. If a horse is being aggressive, like when a mare may be protecting her foal, it is clear our presence has done something to distress the horse. However, there are also more subtle ways our presence can trouble a horse which many people miss because they are not living in the moment with the horse. Here is an example:

I was at a clinic demonstrating a change of direction on a circle with fluidity. Just as I was preparing to ask Cisco to change directions my husband drove up the driveway in our truck and trailer. My horse saw this out the far door of the arena. He also heard the diesel engine long before he saw it.

He perked right up with curiosity, and I totally lost his attention. His ears, eyes, and whole body were completely focused on the arrival of our truck and trailer. I gently reached for the lead rope to bring him back to me. He obeyed, but the second I released he snapped back to his own agenda. I repeated my actions one more time, and so did he.

At that moment I thought about all the principles I have learned. I realized that even though the students were waiting to see the demonstration there was a much more important and pressing matter at hand. Was I willing to sacrifice my time and my agenda to do the right thing for my horse? Or was I going to be rude interrupting his curiosity forcing him to go on with my agenda when at that moment he was clearly in his horse world, not my world.

I can remember plenty of times when I have gone on with my agenda ignoring the mental and emotional state of my horse. I justified this because I felt pressed for time and I was concerned about people watching who might want to keep the show on the road. But this time I decided all of that didn't matter. I needed to take the time it takes, remain cognizant of my horse's world, and not worry about what others were thinking or how much time we had.

I said to everyone, "Cisco is noticeably distracted right now by our truck and trailer. So what's the big deal? Why can't we just let him stand here until he is ready to move on? Let's just wait and see what happens." As I waited, I was wondering what my horse was thinking. If I were a horse I might have been wondering: Why is our trailer coming back? Where did it go? When did it leave? Did Keith go get one of my buddies at home? Am I going home now? I don't know if horses think this way, but we all know our horses recognize the sound of our truck before we pull in the drive-way.

After Keith shut the engine off and walked toward the door, Cisco turned his attention back to me as if to say, "Ok, I'm ready now, thanks for waiting for me." He performed the change of direction on the circle with fluidity. But more importantly with a willing heart!

This was a very simple thing, but if I had ignored my horse's world my presence could have unsettled him. Knowing Cisco he wouldn't have made a big deal out of it. However,
I am glad I was mindful of my horse's world, because later on one of the people watching commented that I had just made a huge deposit in our relationship account.

When we can truly remove our own agenda it will advance our relationship. But we must be willing to live in the moment with the horse allowing him to be a horse. We must also quit expecting them to act and think like us. If we encourage their curiosity, and recognize the simplest things which are important to them, they will accept our presence as a pleasant experience. When we give ourselves permission to take the time it takes, a horse seldom becomes upset with our presence. Resistance, fear, and frustration will eventually become a thing of the past!

First Priority is Dignity of the Horse

The dignity of the horse comes first with a person seeking to win a horse's heart. Although a wholesome self image is vital to a savvy horseman, I believe there is no place for a super-inflated ego in good horsemanship. A healthy self-respect and recognition of our own potential and that of the horse are both significant when putting the dignity of the horse first. It is our job to adjust to fit the situation. No matter what happens, the reality is: Our first priority is to honor the horse by living in the moment with them.

This doesn't mean we should set aside our goals and dreams. We do need some kind of road map to keep us from getting lost. Without guidance we may wander aimlessly on our journey. A horse will do the same without proper guidance because he learns what he lives and he lives what he learns. The effect our daily actions and interactions have on a horse may show up now, and they may not show up until later, but they will show up. Some of us miss the fact the horse is doing just what we have trained him to do. He is what he is. If we think he is stubborn or stupid we are using the wrong word. The horse is ignorant. He is ignorant because of our own lack of experience, timing, focus, and a concrete plan for development. The horse will remain ignorant until we have a progressive program to follow and our skills as a teacher improve.

We have to be paying attention to each moment in order to provide the immediate guidance and strong leadership a horse needs. If we miss this moment the horse will realize we don't have the answers he needs, but Mother Nature does. So he may stop listening to us and start listening to his primal instincts. When this happens the dust is often settling around us before we ever realize it has started and we wonder what just happened.

Every horse owner is a trainer whether they get paid for it or not. The moment we make eye contact with a horse from a distance the training has begun. In fact everyone who holds a lead rope is a trainer. Anyone who handles our horse is training him. This even includes the vet, farrier, and any person who mucks the stall or feeds him. Some of these people do it better than others. There are the chosen few who have a natural inborn talent for horsemanship. However, anyone driven with a great amount of desire and a wholesome self-image can become a great horseman given enough effort, time, instruction, a plan, and experience.

The best horsemen have learned that to live in the moment means we are working on ourselves even more than we are working on the horse. When we choose to work on self we may notice a horse sometimes understands us better than we understand ourselves. If we have an open mind we can allow the horse to show us how to communicate with this same depth of transparency. Working with a horse can cultivate what's best or worst in us. They can change our attitude to the world around us when we remain adaptable.

Horses are PEOPLE EXPERTS because they are thinking, feeling beings with a gift of reading their surroundings, which includes linking to the true emotions of the humans they encounter. Horses don't separate how they feel from how they act. They will tell you exactly where they are at and what they want from you. Every moment with them they are taking your measure with accuracy because their survival depends on it. They react positively to authenticity and negatively to behavior that isn't authentic. Most of us know you can't fool a horse into thinking you aren't afraid when you are. The bottom line is you can't fake it with horses. If you try they will be confused and you will be frustrated. It is a simple fact people act like the sort of person they think they are. It's impossible for them to do otherwise for any period of time, no matter how much willpower they exercise. We may be able to fake it with people some of the time, but horses will recognize every time whether we are being authentic or not because they can judge character with accuracy. With their sensitivity and talent for reflecting our emotions back to us, horses can impart to us profound personal insight when we choose to live in the moment with them. A genuine horseman who has received this kind of illumination from the horse can't help but put the dignity of the horse first because his priority is to win the horse's heart.

A Holistic Approach to Setting Realistic Goals

I have observed so many new horse owners who have lost their original dream when the reality of life with a horse happens. The romantic vision of galloping across the hills as the sun sets and living happily ever after is too often replaced with frustrations, emergency room visits, and a ton of vet, feed, and farrier bills. Some questions a fellow might want to answer before trying to fulfill these dreams are: What are your real reasons for wanting to own a horse? How much time and money do you have to dedicate to this endeavor? Are you willing to seek professional advice and assistance? Are you willing to admit your shortcomings and not blame the horse for everything? How much do you really want to succeed with horses? Are you willing to do what it takes to win a horse's heart? What are you hoping for? How close a match is there between what you are hoping for and reality?

In order to live our horse dreams we must first set realistic goals with appropriate time frames, and feel free to change them anytime. After all they're ours, we made them and we can change them whenever it seems fitting. The average goal aims way too high because we set them high to match our dreams. I'm not suggesting we throw out our dreams, rather

I believe a more realistic and holistic approach will help us be more successful toward living those dreams.

For example; instead of saying "I will canter my horse on a trail ride over the hills as the sun sets." we could say, "I will canter my horse only when we are both ready because we have done the preparation necessary to set us up for success. Then I will go on a trail ride in a familiar environment with another experienced rider who has a calm trail horse. I will progress to longer rides at faster speeds as our confidence and skill builds."

Maybe we should even throw a realistic time frame, for example: By the end of the year. Now we have the entire year to work on this goal and there won't be so much pressure to perform by tomorrow. If we do this, a horse will be more willing because a horse can feel our pressure to hurry up and get something done. When they feel this they can resist even more which can manifest several different ways like: becoming more afraid, shut down, naughty, or obstinate.

Remember the big picture. Most realistic goals are about self-improvement, which includes: Quitting a bad habit, changing the way we look or feel about something, or getting educated on a subject. This requires our mind and body to change, and although it's possible to do a 100% turn around in a short amount of time, it's not very likely.

Chances for success improve with a plan which allows for failure, incorporates both the horse and the person's strengths, and slowly moves toward the overall goal in a way that makes it harder to quit than to keep going. A realistic plan which focuses on the big picture will stack the odds in our favor of living those dreams. Here are several ideas to keep us focused on the big picture.

1. **Break a year into chunks with a theme.**
   Most of us don't have the luxury of an indoor arena, so other than our horse's physical care we don't spend much time with them in the winter. Because of this, January and February would be a good time to get in shape. Start an exercise program so when spring rolls around our riding will be even better as a result of improved physical fitness. Remember riding is an athletic sport, not an activity for couch potatoes. If we want to ride well it takes a great amount of physical agility and this requires some conditioning.

   Even though the entire first couple months of the year might not directly address the ultimate goal, down the line these activities still help achieve the dream. Use imagination to break the rest of the year up into chunks with a theme and it will provide a clear vision, a concrete purpose, consistency and steady strokes of success that will paint the big picture.

2. **Involve family in the big picture.**
   Finding a way to involve family members in the quest will prevent needless trouble when they try to pull us in the opposite direction. If we share our goals with them chances are they will be supportive and do anything we ask, especially when they see how they fit into the big picture.

3. **Include existing strengths and good habits in the big picture.**
   While this may fall in the "duh files" it's surprising how often people ignore their own history. We need to embrace the things we are good at and make sure they are part of the plan. Plus, don't forget to include that which the horse is good at. Take what he offers and mold it into

something which fits into the big picture. Build on your horse's strengths instead of worrying so much about his weaknesses and faults.

It is more important to focus on what we can do and how far we have come rather than on what we still can't do with our horse. Celebrate the baby steps towards a goal.

4.   Find strength in numbers.
Even the most independent of us need support from time to time to help us fill in the blanks of the big picture. Unless the goal is completely off the radar there is support available. Don't try to go it alone. Find a riding buddy or study group with the same principles of horsemanship. Support from a qualified caring professional can keep us on track if the big picture starts to look fuzzy. A good instructor or trainer can often clear up the vision with constructive criticism and encouragement plus inspire the quest for more knowledge. In other words, get educated, and hang out with the right people.

5.   Use the natural power of observation.
The most powerful tool we have as a horseman is our natural power of observation. By observing everything we can which has to do with horses, the big picture will start to come in better focus. Learn by watching, listening, and feeling. A horse is so much better at using his natural power of observation than we are because his self-preservation depends upon it. By becoming more aware of everything around us we will start to know what happens before it even happens, just like horses do. In order to see where things are headed requires you to pay attention to your horse 100% of the time. There can't be any slack in this. Knowing what to do will become

second nature when we start to see the subtle movements and changes in a horse's expression.

Plan and Believe to Live Your Dreams

If you are not making the progress you would like towards your ultimate horse dream it could be because your goals are not clearly defined or realistic enough and you don't have a concrete plan. When you set realistic goals you are taking the first step in a positive overt action toward your dreams. Don't waste time regretting all the goals you failed to set in the past or the dreams you still haven't achieved. By choosing to live in the moment you will be creating a successful future. Ordinary people make promises, but successful, extraordinary people make commitments and live them moment by moment. Make a commitment today to your horse that you will put every ounce of physical and mental energy into the effort to win his heart.

Put a plan into action. Give yourself permission to make mistakes and find new solutions to old problems. Learn as much as you can. Cultivate understanding and have more empathy. Repeat this plan day after day, moment by moment and you will live your dreams if you believe.

You must believe completely in your own ability and in your horse. Do not put all your belief in a trainer or instructor's abilities even though they can and should help. Because it is totally up to you and you alone to make sure your horse has a good life. Believe and accept the responsibility for educating yourself and your horse. Then believe in the rightness of the philosophy you have adopted. Believe in your own ability to make independent observations and decisions. Believe in your ability to read a horse's intention and therefore create correct responses from him with clear communication.

Believe you will win your horse's heart because you have the tools and heart to let it happen.

We will win a horse's heart when we respect a horse enough to live in the moment with him. This means a conscious effort when we enter his world to entirely focus on him and leave behind the stresses and time frames of life. It is this willingness to be there, in the moment, without the future controlling us which allows us to *not* just grab the lead and get something done right now without thinking about whether it is what the horse needs or not. Those who are true to winning a horses heart won't be able to go on cheating horses in this way because this principle is way too important.

JOBE: Always a Winner

Sherry sitting on Jobe, (Dad's pride and joy)
with brother Steve

When I was ten years old Dad bought me my first big horse, a crooked legged sorrel mare named Dixie. She was my first 4-H project. She was a slow, rough riding horse and we needed a ten acre pasture to turn around in. I know we never looked very pretty together because it never felt very good riding her. However, I loved her anyway, just like I loved all of our horses despite their faults. My eye was on my Dad's fast rope horse named Jobe. He was the one I was longing to ride.

Jobe was a big dun gelding with a dorsal stripe, a roman nose and a desire to run fast, stop hard, back quick, follow a cow, turn a steer, change leads with ease, and roll back on a dime.

He would do just about anything one asked him to do except walk. You could say Jobe was a forward-aholic. Speed was the name of the game for him. He was always on the go and a bit on the nervous side. No matter who rode him, he was always a winner. He took many a rider to the winners circle and he did it with unreserved enthusiasm. He won trophies, buckles, ribbons, and money, in calf roping, team roping, steer wrestling, pole bending, goat tying, barrel racing, reining, and even a few wild cow pony races. If there ever was an all-around horse he was it. However, a trail ride was a miserable endeavor on the jigging Jobe unless there were cattle in front of him. I guess he was all business because he was great as long as you gave him a job to do.

Barrel racing on Jobe, Sherry is 12 years old.
(Photographer Jim Svoboda)

People who knew him would say he was a horse with a lot of heart. He gave me his all, and I loved him for that. But I didn't deserve to win this horse's heart. Of all the horses I've known if I could go back and do it over again I would do it a lot different with him. I owe him a great apology for all the unjust ways I treated him. One time I ran Jobe when he was sick and he still won. I thought he was going to cough his lungs out after the run. In the darkness of a rodeo parking lot behind all the action I hugged Jobe's neck as my tears filled his mane, telling him I was sorry and I hoped he would survive. Too often I blamed him for my failures, and then I stole the glory from him when I won, at least in my own mind. I'm sure real horsemen saw through the error in my thinking, recognizing it was all horse, not horsewoman, doing the winning.

As far as competition goals and dreams Jobe took me further than any other horse and he wasn't even my horse. The whole family shared Jobe and even some who weren't related by blood. These friends were part of our horse and rodeo family. Jobe was my Dad's pride and joy. Through his unselfish sharing of his great horse many riders had the privilege of experiencing a horse with a lot of heart. His physical power, strength, and athletic ability beneath you were not overshadowed by his will and enthusiasm to get the job done and win while doing it.

At the age of twelve my wish came true. I started riding Jobe in junior rodeos, gymkhanas, and 4-H competitions when he was fourteen years old. He was a lot of horse for a small girl. I needed a new hat every time I heard the announcer say, "Look at that little girl on that big ol' fast horse." My head and ego grew every time I heard a compliment or won another competition. By the time I was a freshman in high school the dreams of winning were becoming reality. I was on a high and it felt good even though I had an over inflated opinion about myself. When I wasn't on top I was less than fair with Jobe. I not only blamed him for my bad runs but I punished him without mercy. He was always trying but I was blind to the fact that most of the problems we had were my own, not his.

Even though Jobe took me to the winners circle more often than not, I remember my most humiliating moment on him as if it were yesterday. It was my third and final run at the PRCA rodeo in my hometown, Burwell, Nebraska. I had two previous good runs in the big open arena. I decided I was going to show them all what we could really do. So I put on a pair of spurs. Ooops! I since have learned spurs are not so good for making horses go faster, they are really for perfecting lateral moves and such. Anyway, ol' Jobe took offense to my new equipment. As I stabbed him thinking it would make him go faster it shortened him up and we knocked over both the second and third barrels. It was the first time in our career we had knocked over two barrels in one run. I promised myself I would make sure this never happened again as I ran and hid in humiliation with tears streaking down my face.

I learned some important lessons that day about goals, competition, and most of all relationships. I should have trusted Jobe to do what he did best. If I had, I am sure we would have won. But in my greed to be the best and win I sacrificed my relationship with Jobe and he proved to me I was wrong. The situations horses can put us in have a way of taking us down a notch or two just when we are getting a little bit too big for our britches. Though I don't believe a horse has direct thoughts about bringing a person down a notch, this is often the natural consequence. I am thankful for this lesson even though at the time I found it very difficult to muster up the courage to let my face be seen during the rest of the rodeo. When people talked with me about the run, I didn't let my secret out of the bag, because I was too proud to admit I had been wrong. The only one who saw right through my false stories or at least called me on it was my Dad. I had to tell him the truth and he didn't give me a big lecture. However, he did give me the "I told you so look," and I knew he was right.

First year of high school rodeos barrel racing on Jobe.
(Photographer Jim Svoboda)

Jobe never did buck with me nor do anything nasty, but somehow he had a way of putting me in my place when I needed it. Like the time I hopped on him bareback without a bridle out in the pasture. I found out just how fast he could run when I asked him to go. He galloped at lightening speed right back to the barn sliding to a stop in front of a gate shooting me over the top of it. After I got up and shook the dust off, I thought, "Boy, I guess I'll never do that again." This was the second time he had catapulted me over a fence. The first one was during a practice session. He went right by the first barrel hitting the fence of the arena which was followed by a quick, sharp right turn. I didn't make the turn with him, instead I kept going forward right over the fence, landing on the road on the other side.

Jobe was always a winner but he taught me one of the most important lessons in my life: Goals are good and winning isn't everything. He taught me riding is more than winning; it is an art form and a partnership. The art and partnership should come first, and then competition. If I have to sacrifice the relationship, integrity, physical, mental, or emotional health of the horse in order to achieve a goal which is designed to somehow boost my ego or give me monetary gain, then I have digressed from seeking the art form of horsemanship. Thanks to the painful lessons the winner Jobe taught me, I am now on a journey to create my own version of art in horsemanship designed to inspire others to follow their own artistic path of horsemanship where one seeks to protect the partnership above all else.

Winning both barrells and poles at District 4-H on Jobe.
(Photographer Jim Svoboda)

Chapter 3: Partnership vs. Ownership

"Teachers open the door. You enter by yourself." -- *Chinese proverb*

Responsible Horse Care

Anyone who has a horse in their back yard is a horse owner. But just because one holds the papers on a horse doesn't mean they have earned the privilege of partnership. Money can buy the right to ownership but we must win the horse's heart using love and leadership before a true partnership is developed.

Good physical care of a horse is one of the most important responsibilities of ownership and there is a lot involved. Proper nutrition, vaccinations, worming, dental care, hoof maintenance, and providing a safe, comfortable environment is not only time consuming but expensive. No matter how perfect the physical care of a horse is, this alone will not earn enough brownie points to form a lasting partnership. We must also look after the mental and emotional fitness of a horse in order to work our way into a true partnership where trust and respect flow deep.

The term ownership implies "to posses something" like a piece of property which we are responsible to care for, however it also suggests selfishness. Let's face it: Most of us own a horse for some selfish reasons like a nice ride anytime we wish, winning a competition, or maybe even prestige. Once we can set aside some of the selfish desires of ownership our primary focus begins to change. The following are some changes which need to take place for a partnership to form.

Qualifications for a Partnership

- **Privilege:** Riding becomes a wonderful privilege never to be taken for granted.

- **Listening**: Listening to what the horse is trying to tell us becomes more important than blind obedience.

- **Character:** Becoming the right person for a horse takes priority over finding the right horse. Selling a horse is sometimes the right answer, but it usually does not solve all the owner's horse problems. More than one person has sold one horse and ended up having the exact same problems or worse with another horse. I have found the most challenging horses are the ones which taught me the most and helped me address the issues which I needed to change. We often waste too much time looking for the perfect horse instead of becoming the perfect partner for our horse. I have developed the most rewarding relationships with the horses who have challenged me the most to seek help, grow, and change.

- **Understanding**: Resorting to bigger harsher equipment in order to control a horse is replaced with techniques which understand the nature of the horse. Relying on more severe equipment or drugs to control a horse is a crutch for our own inadequacies as a horse handler.

- **Time:** In a partnership there is no such thing as a quick fix to any horse problem. Hurrying will hurt the quality of whatever task we undertake. Mistakes, poor performance, and even injuries come from quick fixes and rushing. If we are not careful they can often create even bigger problems on down the line. We have to start thinking like a problem solver. This may include going backwards first before moving forward at a pace according to the confidence level, ability, and understanding of the horse. In a partnership, timetables for goals are often recalculated based on the needs and abilities of all parties in the relationship.

- **Harmony:** Riding is more than sitting on top of a horse looking good and not falling off. It is about staying connected mentally and allowing harmony. This means we move our body in the same fashion as we expect the horse to move. When we are able to stay out of the horse's way we can influence the horse in a positive way both mentally and physically. To be out of the horse's way physically means we can position our weight on his back so we compliment his balance and maximize his movements. When we learn to find that sweet spot our performance will improve because we will no longer be inhibiting his movements. Without a mental connection, no amount of proper seat and weight position will improve harmony if the horse is scared, unconfident, unwilling, or confused. When we present clear communication (the mental and emotional element) and are able to stay out of the horse's way (the physical element) riding is harmonious and leads to partnership.

This story illustrates staying out of the horse's way even though it was an accident. I was working on cantering with straightness by riding from point A to point B along a fence line. My horse was doing great. She was relaxed with a nice cadence and feeling quite straight. It is significant that there was a grove of trees on the other side of the fence, because all of a sudden I realized there was a branch hanging too low right in front of me which was about to smack me in the face. Knowing it was going to hurt and that I didn't have time to slow my horse down or turn I ducked. As I shifted my weight the reins remained loose. Dolly did a perfect flying lead change in harmony with me like I have never felt her do before. She never missed a beat staying in the same cadence and emotional stability.

I only wish I could reproduce a flying lead change like this every time I ask for one. As I arrived at our point of rest I sat there chewing on what had just happened. I believe the reason it was so good is because it was so natural. There was no force, resistance, or pressure, mental, emotional, or physical. There was only pure harmony of movement between horse and rider. She felt my shift of weight and did in her body exactly what my body had done. I know it was an accident, but it doesn't take away from the feeling it gave me. It reminds me of what I have heard some great trainers say, "Take what the horse offers you and mold it." At that moment I believe my horse took what I offered and blended with me because I was not bracing or being demanding. .

I can get flying lead changes with Dolly, but never with the same ease and comfort experienced that day. The difference may be that she can feel my body start to tense up the moment I think about doing one. This could cause her to believe I am going to slam her into it. This was a real lesson for me on riding in a natural way with fluidity and harmony instead of pressure. If I can retrain my brain to move *into* the lightness instead of *away* from the pressure, I believe I will begin to get better results. I also have to convince Dolly in her mind and emotions that I will do this. This will give her the confidence and feel she needs to do a flying lead change any time I ask, without resistance.

- **Leadership:** As a horse owner it is easy to slip into complacency where one begins to tolerate unsafe behaviors from their horse. In a true partnership unsafe behaviors are not tolerated but are dealt with in a fair, understandable manner. Confident leadership with just the correct amount of assertiveness mixed with kindness will lead to safety. Too much aggression or too much passivity will decrease safety. Love without leadership can cause rebellion, and domination without love can break the spirit of the horse. Taking uncalculated risks with a horse is just plain silly. The horse is dangerous enough without not thinking through situations and allowing for proper preparation which set the horse up for success. When we stop paying attention to behaviors we know are unacceptable we often end up saying, (right after a wreck) "I don't know what happened. There was no warning......"

- **Education**: At the first sign of problems, horse owners often look for a trainer to straighten their horse out. It is wise to reach out for help when things go wrong. A trainer can help us get a good start. But the ultimate success of the horse's long term development is the responsibility of each individual owner. Sending the horse off to get fixed is a good idea when we lack the skill to help the horse, especially with a young horse and an inexperienced rider. However, without the owner being involved in the solution and transformation this will only put a band-aid on the problem.

Training for both the horse and human together is essential for long term success. All too often a trainer does a great job with the horse, but back in the hands of the owner the same problems arise if the owner isn't educated alongside the horse. In order to keep the horse tuned up the owner must also be tuned up. If they are tuned up together the chances of a harmonious relationship increase. In a partnership, first we have to quit blaming the horse, and then we need to be willing to look in the mirror and accept responsibility for the problems we have with the horse.

BEWARE! Not everyone who hangs out a horse trainer shingle is qualified to teach you and your horse to become partners. A person doesn't have to get a license to charge money for horse training. There are no standards in the industry. I have heard many horror stories of unsuccessful experiences where a person gets the horse back from a trainer with a big fat bill and the advice to sell the horse because he is un-trainable. Or worse yet, the horse winds up with more bad habits than when you sent him to the trainer, or is injured.

If a trainer will not allow you to drop by and observe your horse in training then you may want to ask why the trainer doesn't want you around. What are they hiding? Ask the trainer in a tactful way why this is his or her policy. Even if you are satisfied with their answer, I would still politely ask to schedule a time at the trainer's convenience at least once a week to check on the horse's progress. Be sure to ask questions about what you should be learning while the horse is in school. Above all else, avoid telling the trainer how to do his job. After all, you hired a trainer because you believe he knows more about developing a horse or solving problems than you do.

The ultimate trainer is one who includes you in the process so you know what to do with the horse when you get him home. Not all trainers are good with people. So if the trainer doesn't want to teach you, ask the trainer for their recommendation of an instructor with a similar philosophy to help you continue the hard work the trainer has put into the horse. There are a lot of good, reputable trainers in the basket with a few bad apples. So choose a trainer with care by asking for recommendations and don't just go with the cheapest one.

- **Communication:** Knowing the right techniques and tricks of the trade are not effective without a communication system based on a language the horse understands. Body language based on feel is the primary means of communication for the horse. Therefore we need to learn to use our body and expressions in a way that makes sense to the horse. Communication using a language based on respect, trust, and listening which can flow both ways is a cornerstone for any good partnership.

- **Responsibility:** Horse ownership has many responsibilities, and a partnership is not for irresponsible, shallow, selfish, or greedy people. It takes a very responsible, compassionate, humble, and wise person to become a worthy partner who is able to win a horse's heart.

  The first responsibility is to get educated before one buys a horse. Through my own experience I have come across many first-time horse owners who are at the point of getting rid of their horse even if it means giving it away for free. They are in this predicament because horse ownership turned out to be way more than they bargained for. They found out too late that they weren't equipped to deal with it. I only wish these people would have asked for help sooner or, even better, were educated before they ever purchased a horse. That way, these stories would no doubt have better endings for both the horse and the human.

The second responsibility is to commit to the best physical, mental, and emotional care of the horse no matter what it costs. Believe me when I say it will be expensive in money, time, and effort. Horse care is not for the lazy or a person already struggling financially. Horse ownership is a serious responsibility because the horse is one hundred percent reliant on us for his well being. We should not let them down, and anyone who does is not worthy of winning a horse's heart.

It is unfortunate when horses are subjected to conditions and practices which cause lameness, starvation, and even death because of ignorant or irresponsible owners. It is hard to believe, but because of the flood of unwanted horses on the market today there are reports of people leaving horses at sale barns. Horse rescue organizations cannot keep up with the numbers and the finances involved in saving so many unwanted, neglected, or abused horses are never ending.

One of my students recently called me with a story about her neighbor who bought a trailer load of foals and yearlings at a sale for $5 a piece. She called me to get the number of a nearby horse rescue because these horses were dying through starvation. This is just one tragic story among many. However, the root of the problem is not only irresponsible horse owners it is too many horses on the market for the current demand. This supply and demand problem has various causes which can be debated for many hours among horse owners, which brings me to the third responsibility.

The third responsibility is wise decisions about birth and death which consider the quality of life for the horse as a first priority. Before breeding a mare, each horse owner should ask themselves a few questions:

1. What kind of partnership will be available for this foal?
2. If I can't find a good home for this foal, can I afford to keep and feed another horse for the duration of his life?
3. Will this be a quality foal which will be desirable to others?
4. Is this an emotional or financial decision?
5. If it is emotional; do I really need another horse?
6. If you do need or want another horse would it be better to buy one which needs a partner now and can meet your expectations?
7. If it is financial; is it a reasonable risk that I will be able to sell this horse at a profit?
8. Is there a true market for this kind of horse at the price I need?
9. If I can't sell the horse as a young untrained horse, am I willing to put in the time, effort,

and money to develop the horse into a riding horse which may be more desirable for a larger market?

10. Am I knowledgeable about raising a foal from birth until he is a dependable riding horse years later? If not, am I willing to seek out and pay for the necessary professional help in order to be successful?

If a person cannot answer these questions honestly and meet these challenges, then perhaps bringing another horse into this world should be reserved for professionals who are educated and have the proper facility and finances to support responsible breeding practices. I am not suggesting anyone should stop breeding horses. Rather we should carefully examine our motives and ability to ensure quality life for the foals we produce according to the demands of the current market. The price of a horse in today's market is based on the cost of sperm, desirability of the horse, and the price of horse flesh or meat (or the lack thereof.)

In today's horse industry most horses are purchased for enjoyment and entertainment rather than a commodity to be raised specifically for slaughter and consumption, such as cattle, hogs, and chickens. Therefore our motives and attitudes toward reproduction and sales are much different from this type of consumable market.

Breeding too many horses leads us to the topic of death and how to handle unwanted or unusable horses. There are many ways to deal with this problem and each person has their opinion on what solutions are acceptable and which ones are not. If we are a people with compassion and principles which recognize the seriousness of our responsibility to care for the horse in birth and death then our practices will be shaped by those principles. The question we must continually ask ourselves is: Are we doing what is best for the horse? If we can say yes to this question then we are the kind of person who can win a horse's heart and are worthy to be called a partner.

Cooperation, Joint Rights, and Responsibilities

A partnership involves close cooperation between two parties having specified joint rights and responsibilities. In the dictionary another meaning for partner is "one of the heavy timbers that strengthen a ship's deck to support a mast." This is a very descriptive analogy of what it means to be a partner to a horse. We need to be dependable and consistent in order to strengthen a horse's confidence. When a horse is confident in us as a worthy partner then they will return the favor. The bottom line is a horse who has become a partner knows his responsibilities and job. He can perform these without any fear or tension while looking happy and magnificent. When a horse becomes your partner, ownership takes on a whole new meaning and the only prize worth winning is your horse's heart. Fame and fortune may be a natural result of this kind of partnership but it won't be top priority. Live like a partner with your horse for one day and then let it be a pattern for all the days of life and you will win your horse's heart forever.

GYPSY My Very Own Horse

Gypsy and Sherry all dressed up.

Even though I had several horses before Gypsy she was the first horse I could really call my own. Prior to her I rode a lot of other horses, but I always had to share them with other family members. Gypsy was different because she was mine and mine alone. After Ginger she became my second true partner. Dad took me to my first horse auction. It was so exciting looking at all the pens of horses. One little strawberry roan filly had my name written on the white blaze of her forehead. She was a wild little thing and her four white stockings were a blur as she pranced and ran around the pen. She wasn't even halter broke. I didn't care because she was the one I wanted. To me she was exotic and exuberant, plus full of life and spirit just like me.

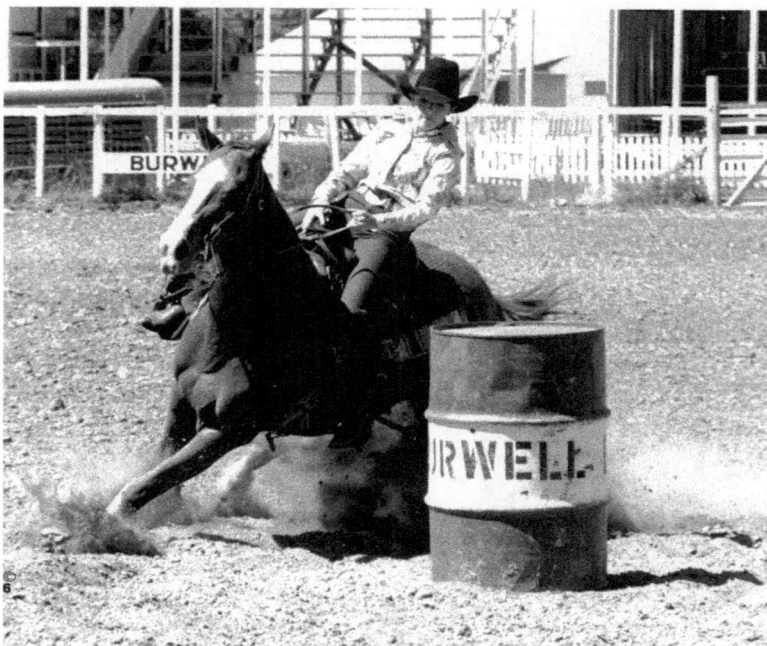

High School Rodeo, Sherry at 18 yrs. old on Gypsy 6 yrs. old
(Photographer Jim Svoboda)

When the bidding started I was so nervous. I was even more surprised when I got the bid for only $100. I was in the seventh grade and ready to prove myself by training my first horse alone from the start. I wouldn't recommend buying an un-started filly for most thirteen year olds. But remember I had been riding horses since I was four years old and I had also helped my dad start other colts.

My first job was to catch this splendid strawberry roan. I soon found out this wasn't as easy as I thought it would be. I spent a lot of time hanging out with her in her special corral trying to make friends. It was puzzling to me why she was so afraid of me because I was only trying to pet her. Didn't she understand I wanted to be her friend? All I knew was I wanted to touch her and she didn't want to be touched. I tried bribing her with food, trapping her, chasing her, and even roping her. I don't remember what finally worked. I do know this, retreat was not part of my strategy. The poor horse may have had to give it up because of my persistence. I didn't know what I was doing, but I did know giving up was not an option. This was my horse and I wasn't going to fail. It was a miracle that somehow we became partners. It is still a mystery to me why this little filly full of flight response and skepticism about humans would find a way to trust me.

I spent the first year with Gypsy grooming, feeding, and loving on her. Anytime we are not in the saddle we are doing some fashion of ground work even if it is not a prescribed program with specific exercises. How we interact with a horse when we are not on his back will develop the relationship either in a constructive or harmful way, whether we are consciously aware of it or not. When done well proper ground work methods with a definite purpose in mind will advance the relationship with a horse in a productive manner. I didn't know one thing about formal ground work. However, I remembered seeing some people on TV in fancy English saddles with pretty jackets and cute black velvet helmets doing something they called longe-lining. I thought it was so cool. I decided to try to teach Gypsy to circle around me, but it never happened. I spent a lot of time running circles around her while she kept hiding her hinny from me with a puzzled look on her face. No matter how hard I tried all I could get her to do was face me. What a funny site that must have been. I bet the neighbors got a few laughs out of watching me. I finally gave up and resorted to what was familiar to me, riding! I knew I could ride almost anything with hair. So I gave up this notion about official ground work. It would be almost twenty-five years later before I would become skillful with horses on the ground. I have since discovered there is so much more to expert horsemanship than riding. The best horsemen are just as good on the ground as they are at riding.

Sherry and Gypsy in the Nebraska
Rodeo Queen Contest 1976

When Gypsy was two years old, I just hopped on her one day and started riding like I had been doing it for years. For some reason I expected it would be easy, and it was. The only way I can account for this success is that we must have had the makings of a true partnership or maybe it was just dumb luck. I would like to think that by this time I didn't just own Gypsy she was a part of me and I was a part of her.

I started experimenting with using leg cues and shifting my weight to change directions and gaits. I had never done this before and nobody taught me. However I did read about it in an article in my favorite magazine, "Western Horseman". I was able to ride her with more harmony than any other horse I had ever ridden. Sometimes it seemed effortless. One of our favorite things to do after a training session was to ride down to the river galloping as fast as she could run. I was a mere passenger, trusting her every step of the way to not trip and then to stop before we got to the road. One hot day after our gallop I rode her into the river to cool off. She stepped into a soft sandy spot where we started to sink. When she lay down I jumped off and started screaming at the top of my lungs to get her up. I was sure we were in quick sand and she would never get out. All I could think about was loosing my partner. Thankfully after a struggle we both got out. We never went back there again.

I was so proud of Gypsy. For a long time I wouldn't let anyone else ride my own special horse. She was my project and my best friend. I didn't want to share the special bond we had with anyone else as if sharing it might break it.

Thanks to all the lessons Gypsy taught me I learned about the responsibilities and hard work of ownership plus the importance and blessings of partnership. I learned what it means to be dedicated to goals and at the same time committed to a relationship. Even though I was competing on her by the time she was four, the most rewarding moments I had with her were those early days of developing our partnership. I know I made mistakes with her because my training techniques were crude and sometimes non-existent. This fact didn't always seem critical because what I did have going for me was an attitude of justice, kindness, and patience which went a long way to winning the heart of a wild little strawberry roan filly named Gypsy.

High School Rodeo State Finals, Sherry at 17 yrs old on Gypsy 5 yrs. old
(Photographer Jerry Gustafson)

Chapter 4: Knowledge vs. Frustration

"Everything should be made as simple as possible, but not one bit simpler." -- Albert Einstein

Tears of Frustration or the Joy of Effectiveness

Very few horse owners make money with horses. To most of us it is a financial drain and we have to sacrifice a lot in order to have one of these beautiful creatures in our lives. Then why do we own them? Some of the reasons may include: Adventure, thrill of an adrenaline high, satisfaction of winning a competition, socialization, camaraderie with other horse lovers, a symbol of wealth and prestige, work, or to get a job done. Other factors may not be as apparent, like, a person likes to learn, whether they know it or not, or craving a spiritual bond. Whatever value you hold dearest, the most popular reason may be FUN!

It is true the majority of horses today are considered a hobby, not a necessity. I know there are those who will argue vehemently with me about this term 'hobby', because some people are so passionate about horses. To many of us they are a way of life. Others cannot imagine life without them. In fact, I would categorize myself in this adoring bunch, because we have ten horses and none of them are for sale for any price. This sounds illogical to anyone in the horse business, therefore my point. I'm not trying to make money with my horses otherwise they would be a commodity, not a part of our family. So whether you agree with my language or not, most people in America own a horse for enjoyment.

As I observe horse people at events I have discovered how many are frustrated. When the human is frustrated most often the horse is also. I've seen people to the point of tears because they couldn't communicate their desires to the horse. They tell stories about fights they have with their horse. I hear over and over about all their horse problems, wrecks, injuries, and destroyed confidence. Yet somehow they still want to find a way to live the dream.

When did we start thinking frustration, fears, fighting, problems, wrecks, and injuries were fun? We all know these are real issues and they are not fun, not to mention they can become very expensive. We all know these problems weren't part of the original dream of galloping off into the sunset. I am not judging anyone with these issues because I too have been frustrated to the point of tears. I've fought with horses which led to wrecks and injuries. I have accepted undesirable and unsafe behaviors as normal. I learned to put up with these behaviors because I didn't know what to do about them.

I have wanted to win so bad that in order to satisfy my own ego I subjected horses to unfavorable practices and conditions without consideration of their needs. I have blamed my horse for my poor performance thinking he was mean, naughty, stubborn, or stupid. I am now aware that most of the time the horse wasn't any of those things. They just didn't understand, were nervous, afraid, or unconfident.

There is a vicious cycle of frustration in this kind of mistaken thinking which goes something like this. First the human has poor communication skills, so the horse doesn't understand what is expected of him. When the horse doesn't understand he doesn't respond properly. Then the human gets frustrated because the horse didn't do the right thing. This causes his communication to be even less understandable. Therefore the horse gets more frustrated and on it goes over and over, until either someone gives up or gets hurt. I'm sure there are other explanations for why people get frustrated with horses and horses get frustrated with people. But if true horsemanship is *feel* than this concept of being understood is imperative.

The failure rate of new horse owners who end up getting out of horses altogether, and the number of throw-away horses deemed as un-trainable or unsafe, thus unusable, are proof of this cycle of frustration. There are enough sad stories to show that many horse people are far from working in harmony with their equine friends. If we ask the question, "Why am I getting the results I am getting?" we will begin to understand the horse is just giving us feedback and an honest opinion.

If we hear our voice saying, "That dumb horse!" remember, we may be the one making the mistakes. A better thing to say might be, "Wow, that didn't work, I wonder how I could present this to my horse in a different way in order to get a better outcome?"

When a horse is providing us with less than positive feedback it becomes very easy to stick a label on the horse. When we start calling a horse mean, naughty, stubborn, stupid, or moody it can be very injurious towards how we think of the horse. Blaming or excusing the horse for his nature won't solve the problem. We should take seriously any negative feedback our horse gives us and listen to it. This kind of feedback should lead us to examine the effectiveness of our communication. More often than not what people label as a negative personality trait is really just the horse finding a way to escape a situation which is uncomfortable at best and intolerable at worst.

I believe horses do have individual personalities, and we have to learn to work with their inborn characteristics. Something I learned from one of my teachers seems appropriate here. This expression articulates a solution to this frustrating cycle of blame and misunderstanding. If it wasn't effective, it wasn't understood. If a horse doesn't understand, he is confused. When a horse is confused, he can easily become afraid. The proof something was understood is when it is effective.

If we are able to accept our mistakes and shortcomings we will be able to let go of our defensive behaviors and become better horsemen for our horses. When we throw away the useless idea that mistakes are somehow bad we can begin to learn more useful and effective principles which will result in rapid positive progress. Every mistake we make brings us closer to harmony with horses if we are willing to learn from them. Remember it is rare when things are either right or wrong, or good or bad in horsemanship. Everything is either appropriate for the situation or not useful to our goals.

By acknowledging our role in the horse's response and recognizing our mistakes we will break down defensive barriers instead of building them. When the defensive barriers are gone we will be able to see more clearly where the horse is having trouble. Then we will be able to uncover creative solutions to any problem causing frustration.

In summary, if we want to discover new solutions to old problems we must:
- Maintain a perspective where we are responsible for the outcomes and responses a horse give us.
- Keep an attitude of humility.

- Accept mistakes as learning opportunities.
- Remove defensive behaviors where everything is either right/wrong or good/bad

By recognizing our defensive behaviors and replacing these with positive progressive knowledge and self-control the relationship with our horse will develop into a partnership where we can win a horse's heart.

Defensive Horse Behaviors and Remedies

Many of the labels we chose to hang on our horses are really defensive behaviors. We must first be able to recognize defensive behaviors before we can deal with them. The main cause of defensive behavior for most people stems from the fear of making mistakes, being wrong, feeling stupid, or looking incompetent. Because a person doesn't want to look bad they tend to blame the horse when things are not going well. When a human feels he has to defend being right they often replace calm, confident leadership with anger, frustration, or even stronger unfair tactics towards the horse. The human gets sucked into a win/lose battle with the horse instead of being flexible until they find a better way to communicate with the horse.

Here are some common "Defensive Behaviors" horses display and a remedy to each one:

Defensive Behaviors: Disrespectful, Pushy, Dominant, Mouthy

This is one of the most common labels given to horses. A horse will lack respect for the human who is not a good leader. A disrespectful horse is testing the mental fitness of the rider as a leader. Once a horse has granted enough trust to accept the human as a herd member the one big question every horse has is, "Where does this human fit in the pecking order?" If we are not more emotionally, mentally, and physically fit and balanced than our horse we will rank lower.

Remedy: Understand the horse's nature and needs. Then protect your space.

The common remedy of dominating the horse or making the horse submit with force, fear, intimidation, and pain is seldom the answer. You may gain his attention but not his true respect. Only fair and just leaders gain our true respect. On the other hand we can't love a horse into respect either.

Working with a horse's true nature and meeting his individual needs is the only thing that ultimately earns the horse's vote for your leadership. This means learning to be as soft as possible yet as firm as necessary depending on the situation. Become more interesting to this horse and keep him moving. Don't let him move you around. Every time you move him out of your space you move up in rank.

Defensive Behaviors: Aggressive, Dangerous, Mean, Unpredictable, Explosive

As prey animals horses are naturally defensive. Their first instinct for self-preservation is flight or escape. However, sometimes when they are pushed hard enough, or if their genetics are right, they decide the best defense is a good offense. When a horse takes an offensive position to defend his space he is simply expressing an extroverted behavior of defensiveness rooted in mistrust, disrespect, or both. This is usually caused by over aggressive handlers who may also be reacting out of a defensive behavior rooted in fear.

Remedy: A calm, focused leader who can balance firmness with friendliness.

An extroverted, aggressive horse needs clear, firm, and absolutely consistent boundaries for acceptable and unacceptable behavior. Again this means learning to read the horse and the circumstance so you know when to be soft and when firmness is required and how much. What firmness means to one horse is not firmness to another, depending on their inborn nature. Interrupt their habits and patterns by constructively redirecting their energy.

Defensive Behaviors: ADD, No Attention Span, Naughty, Spooky, Wayward

A horse with these behaviors is often trying to use mental distraction to cope with things. By focusing on anything but the rider the horse can avoid interaction. These horses are often tense, unpredictable, and have a tendency to freeze then explode. These horses are often misread. Most of the time the purpose of their defensive behaviors are to shut us out, much like a teenager who pretends they don't hear what we are saying.

Remedy: Stay focused. Slow down, way down. Take time and use repetition.

A mentally distracted or disassociated horse needs help learning to focus on simple things. They need all the time and repetition it takes to process and accept new information. Slow down by taking the time it takes with them and they will reward your effort. They need their thoughts politely interrupted and redirected as this helps them learn to focus. Sometimes it may feel like you have to do things a million times before they get it, but hang in there. They need your strong focus and patience to keep them on track. Sometimes the best thing to do with them is nothing for quite a while until they become confident and curious enough to want to engage with us.

Defensive Behaviors: Lazy, Stupid, Stubborn, Dull, Sullen, Unmotivated, Bored

This horse is choosing the route of introversion to escape from the rider. They go away mentally and emotionally in order to cope with the situation. These horses are generally not afraid of people. They can be disobedient when they are left-brained (the thinking/learning side of the brain) and un-confident when right-brained (the instinctual/ reactive side of the brain). These horses have a tendency to buck because they don't want to go forward. This horse can outlast most people. They simply stay non-responsive until you give up.

Remedy: Become more interesting, pique their curiosity, and use variety.

An introverted horse needs to be drawn out into freedom of expression. This may mean you need to allow more mistakes, or ask the horse to figure out some things for himself. It is also good to allow some time for this horse to move freely and imperfectly without a rider. Don't be fixated on perfecting a maneuver. Expecting perfection makes them act up because they are confident, fast learners when using the thinking left-side of their brain. Whatever you do, don't drill this horse. Instead use creativity with obstacles and think of playful things to do.

Defensive Behaviors: Fearful, Frantic, Panicky, Crazy, Hypersensitive, Ballistic, Nervous, Hot, Over-reactive

These horses are considered dangerous because they don't have self-control. They have a lot of trouble learning because they use the reactive right-side of their brain most of the time instead of the learning left-side. They have difficulty with anything new. They do not deal well with change. These horses are just trying to cope by utilizing the flight mechanism nature has provided, and they lack trust for the rider. Hot blooded horses are often left in a state of perpetual fear because people think they don't have the ability to work in a calm, focused manner.

Remedy: Make things simple. Use consistency. Ensure the horse he will be safe and comfortable in your presence. Prove you are trustworthy so the horse can relax.

A super-fearful horse needs simplicity and consistency to the point of boredom until it finally feels safe enough to relax. A very fearful horse needs a lot of approach and retreat. More retreat than approach. Don't push them past thresholds or you will blow their confidence in you, themselves, and the situation. Repetition will be your friend with this horse because change scares them. So go slow to help them feel safe and comfortable. Once you get them to relax and trust you there isn't anything they won't do for you.

If we adopt a balanced approach, we can distinguish what the horse needs in order to help him drop the defensive behaviors so he starts wanting to work with us. It is up to us to discover the heart of the problem. Is the horse imbalanced? If so, is the imbalance manifesting in the emotional, mental or physical realm? Balancing a horse's behaviors has many facets and by using the remedy ideas listed above we can begin to break through the various defense mechanisms of the horse. There is no need to label a horse into a certain category because he acts a particular way one day. The same horse may act a different way on another day as the circumstances or environment change. Some days a horse may wake up on the wrong side of the corral, so be prepared for mood changes, especially in mares during hormonal cycles. When we have the correct knowledge about horse behavior and have developed the ability to read horses according to what is happening at each particular moment we won't be tempted to write the horse off by putting him into a particular category.

Remember every day is a new day and you may have a different horse from time to time according to external circumstances. The better prepared you are to handle each situation the less you will be tempted to blame or label your horse.

Recognizing negative behavior as a defense mechanism in the horse allows us to offer a more effective way to interact with a horse which removes a lot of frustrations. When we become effective it also leads to joy in horsemanship because it will assure the way to winning a horse's heart.

Knowledge: A Best Friend or Worst Enemy

Gaining correct knowledge is another way to break this cycle of frustration and win your horse's heart. Knowledge is one of the most powerful tools we possess. It can be our best friend or our worst enemy. It is the reason behind our incompetence or excellence. I have heard other clinicians say "You can lead some people to knowledge, but you can't make them think." Knowledge involves thinking.

Just because we have a brain doesn't mean we are mindful. Every person's brain is as unique as their fingerprints. The brain is continually revising itself throughout life. Our habitual thought patterns can be beneficial or harmful. They can determine our success or our failures. In order to apply the knowledge given to us we must expand and develop our thinking skills and watch with care our habitual patterns of thinking, revising them as needed.

The last area of the brain to reach maturity is the prefrontal cortex where we make social judgments, weigh alternatives, plan for the future, and hold our behavior in check. No matter how much book knowledge we have about any one subject it does not guarantee our success in applying that knowledge effectively in a real life situation. This may be one of the reasons behind our frustration, because there is not one cookie cutter method to training every horse. In our mind we think we know what to do because we read about the technique or someone told us this would work. But when we try it without the thinking skills which allow us to make quick judgments, weigh alternatives, and make new plans according to the situation, the result is mediocre at best and failure at worst. Until a person develops the ability to figure things out for himself and actually understands the horse, they are going to have problems. We must have the ability to make judgments or plans, weigh alternatives, and hold our behavior in check if we want to become a wise horseman who can win a horse's heart.

Think, Have a Plan, Develop Solutions

The lesson here is to learn all we can about quality horsemanship principles, because this knowledge will take us to the other side of frustrations. But remember this: Knowledge must be accompanied with practical thinking skills in order for it to work. I can hear Ray Hunt's voice over and over at a clinic saying, "Think, have a plan." He kept making us think about things, especially from the horse's point of view. He always answered our questions with honesty yet in a way which triggered us to figure some of it out on our own. I think he was trying to empower us with the ability to think deeper about what we were doing and why.

As a teacher, one of my primary goals for students is not only to impart knowledge but to inspire a quest for *more* knowledge. When I teach I don't just see a horse or a person. I envision things they can do together. I don't look at the problems, rather I think of solutions. I don't focus on the destiny. I see the journey and the quest for knowledge which will lead to fewer and fewer frustrations until they are transformed into fascination. It can become very fascinating to try to figure out why a horse did the wrong thing and then find a different and more effective way to communicate to the horse so he does the right thing.

The study of true horsemanship through *feel* has inspired an insatiable hunger in me for more and more knowledge about horses, humans, relationship, and behaviors. I started out with a desire to learn enough training techniques to be able to handle any horse. I ended up with a whole lot more knowledge about life.

A Teachable Heart with a Desire for Change

One of the most important things I have learned in my own personal study is that we can't take in new information about "How to be" until we are aware of and comfortable with "How we are." Change can throw us in turmoil but change is the only way I know to become a better horseman who can win a horse's heart. You wouldn't be reading this if you weren't seeking some answers about how to be a better horseman. If we are exploring and asking questions then we are in the frame of mind conducive to learning. When we choose this process of learning we realize we have to examine ourselves, which is not always pleasant. The changes required to become great horsemen will be even more difficult. We are not in danger of failing until we stop asking questions and think we know it all.

We may have to redefine what horsemanship means to us. Maybe we don't just "do" horsemanship; rather we "are" horsemanship. It is about developing ourselves because horses have a great way of holding us accountable for the "way we are". They are the perfect ones to transform us because they reflect back to us our deepest truths and at the same time our darkest demons. The question is: Do we care enough about our horse to change or do we just own the horse as our slave for entertainment and expect him to do all the changing?

Horsemanship is so individual and personal that perhaps it is something we become. Each person will face their own issues and dig deep into places within themselves they may not even know exist. At times it will be gut wrenching. There's a whole lot more to horsemanship than throwing a leg over and riding off into the sunset if you want to become a great horseman and win your horse's heart. Remaining teachable with a desire for knowledge will take you closer and transform frustrations into gratifying experiences.

SLICK: A Road of Brokenness

Sherry and Slick as a weanling in Twin Bridges, MT

If there ever was a horse that pushed me to the limit and frustrated me to the point of wanting to pull out my hair, it was Slick. On the other hand if there ever was a horse that saved my life from destruction it was the same horse, whom I never understood while he was alive. As I look back, I realize he fully understood me much better than I ever knew myself. Slick healed my broken heart more than once and then broke it once again when he died.

The first time I saw the little bay colt it was June. He was only a few days old. He was standing on the meadow near the Loup River with his dam, Lisa (my Dad's mare). He had a dreadful case of scours. After catching him Dad led him to the river where he held him in the water while I tried to give him a shot of antibiotic in the rump. When he bucked I broke off the needle resulting in penicillin spraying everywhere. This is how most of the rest of our life together went. I fumbled, he resisted and things seldom got better. That broken needle was the beginning of a road of brokenness for both of us.

After Slick was weaned my brother brought him to Montana where I was living. I found a ranch nearby to board him. I played around with him until he was two years old. He was fun and we seemed to get along fine. Due to a move to Nevada, I left Slick behind for a while. In the mean time we hired someone to start riding him. Before we were able to bring him to live with us in Nevada he got tangled in a barbed wire fence, cutting his front foot. It was a severe injury which never healed well. I thought Slick was only hurt physically, but it didn't take long to discover he also had other scars which were mental and emotional. I suppose some of them were due to the treatment he received when I left him behind. I always felt bad about that part of our relationship. I don't blame anyone else because I'm sure they were doing the best they could at the time with the knowledge they had.

During the medical treatment for the injury on his foot he was eared down quite a bit. When he finally came to live with me again I couldn't even begin to touch his ears. Bridling him was out of the question without taking the bridle apart each time. I did so out of frustration and lack of knowledge about how to fix the problem.

The first time I rode him it was like he had never been ridden. He felt like a bottle rocket about ready to go off. I can't believe I crawled on his back in a pasture with no preparation. I'm real lucky I never got hurt on him. Blissful ignorance can sometimes take you through a situation, but sooner or later it will catch up with you.

As the years went by I rode Slick all over the mountains and high desert lands of Nevada and later Wyoming with our two goat friends, Thistle and Petunia. Since I couldn't afford another horse at the time I had a couple of goats for his companions. It was funny when the antelope would spot the threesome. In their curiosity they used to chase us. Slick thought for sure the antelope were going to eat us, but Thistle and Petunia trotted alongside us without alarm.

Slick as a two year old before he was injured in a fence.

Slick never did get over being ear shy. He had a lot of other bad habits that I ignored instead of dealing with them. One time some guys literally winched him into a trailer. Poor Slick was so banged up I sat and cried for hours. I only fell off Slick once and he ran away with me a couple of times. Now I grasp that he was a very unconfident horse because he was always spooky. Due to my lack of knowledge, I misunderstood Slick, becoming an avoid-aholic when it came to the behaviors I couldn't control or fix.

Although I had less harmony with Slick than any other horse I had ridden, I'm sure I rode him more miles of trails than any other. I saw a lot of beautiful scenery from his back. More importantly, for over fifteen years Slick was the main man in my life. He helped me survive two major relationship break ups. From his back I made a lot of difficult decisions as I was searching to find my purpose and place in this world. He was the one constant in my life. I'm sure he knows more about me than any other being on the planet. Because of the many frustrations we had together I don't know if I ever won his heart. If one was to judge by our performance I don't think we would have passed the test. No matter what, this horse was a survivor and taught me how to do the same.

I rode him out into the desert more than once not wanting to ever turn around and go back to my life. He was my escape from reality, yet he always brought me back with a better perspective about my life and who I was. Many a day I saddled him up with the intention to just keep riding out into the desert until I was either lost or could go no further. When that horse would turn back toward home against my will it caused me to ride back into the truth of my life and face it with new strength. During this very unsettled time in my life, I left a lot of things behind, but no matter where I went I always found a way to take Slick and my saddle along with me.

I have noticed that every horse I have had in my life was there at the right time to teach me the lessons I was ready for and needed to learn whether I liked it or not. When the student is ready the teacher will arrive. Slick was not there to teach me about horsemanship techniques as I was not ready and open to learn more about them until after he was gone. Slick taught me about who I really was. Somehow along the way I had lost that. He also taught me to persevere and forgive.

The day Slick died was an agonizing day for me because I lost a remarkable horse that had always been there for me when I needed him, even though I wasn't always able to do what was best for him because of my own ignorance. Somehow during the night a gate was left open where I was boarding him. The gate separated Slick and a mustang which had not yet been tamed or socialized into the herd. This open gate led to a tragic event. It must have been a terrible battle, and Slick lost. The day that gate was left open was a very dark day for both Slick and me because he couldn't survive the injuries he sustained and I lost my best friend. I thought I would never stop crying when we found him in the morning standing in a dark stall with two broken legs. I can't imagine the pain he was in as I looked into his soft eyes which were blurring. I can't imagine how helpless he must have felt.

Riding Slick in the desert of Nevada
letting him bring me back home

When I called my Dad on the phone it is a miracle he understood a word I said because I was sobbing uncontrollably. Of course, he knew what to do and told me I had to put Slick down. I knew he was right and there was no way the bones sticking out of his legs could be repaired, but I still didn't want to let him go. I cut a piece of his mane off before we put the dirt over him and I still have his lock of hair. It had never hurt so bad to lose a horse. I cried for days, and I still get a tear in my eye when I think about the special horse Slick, who helped heal my heart and then broke it again when he passed away.

Sherry and Slick just a few days before he died

At the time my grief was so heavy I couldn't see another horse in my future. I also couldn't appreciate the fact that the day he died was a new beginning for me. It was as if the slate had been wiped clean. Slick had brought me through some tough and troublesome times in my life and a new chapter in my life was about to open. A chapter when I would learn more about horses and myself than I ever dreamed possible. A time of renewal and limitless opportunities arrived where frustrations with horses would become a thing of the past. With a new-found knowledge, the things which used to frustrate me would become rewarding investigations. The journey I had traveled with Slick led me back to recapture the dreams I had while riding Ginger in a natural way as a little girl, untouched by a road of brokenness. Now I am living those dreams as I try to win one horse's heart at a time in a natural way.

Chapter 5: Attitude vs. Tools & Techniques

"The greatest discovery of my generation is that a human being can alter his life by altering his attitudes of mind." --
Williams James

Too Lenient, Too Strict, and Just Right

Who we are is as important as the knowledge we claim to possess. It took me a long time to discover this significant idea. Knowledge without the correct attitude can be a recipe for disaster. It is called wisdom when knowledge and a proper attitude are united in a joint effort toward application of principles. The principles of horsemanship with *feel* can transform our way of thinking by providing us with the knowledge and change of attitude necessary for us to become better horsemen who can win a horse's heart.

Attitude is everything. Without a positive, progressive attitude all the proper tools and techniques can still fail. The way we approach a horse brings out the life in him to connect with us. The correct approach will ensure the horse can understand and respond to what the person asks him to do with confidence while still maintaining his safety and dignity.

Take for example the simple exercise of backing a horse. A person who is too lenient can be so ineffective with it the horse either ignores them or gets irritated. A person who is too strict can border on cruelty or abuse, causing the horse to distrust and become afraid. Even though both people may be using the same technique, their approach is very different because of their attitudes toward the horse and the purpose of the task. However, their results are similar: A confused horse who doesn't respect the human and has lost his desire to perform with exuberance. The horse often knows the intentions and attitudes of the human better than they do. It is only the savvy horseman who knows just how soft or assertive he needs to be so the horse can understand and respond with enthusiasm. When any technique is performed with the proper attitude, timing, *feel,* and release it will produce a willing horse and therefore win his heart.

Doing Less Than it Takes and Quitting Too Soon

Let's look a little more into the horse handler who thinks they can win their horse's heart by kindness alone. The truth is that when they are too lenient a horse barely recognizes this person as even being in the corral with them because they aren't in the horse's consciousness. The horse may also perceive them as an inconvenience or an impediment standing between him and whatever he wants to do. It is not surprising when the horse either ignores this ineffective person, runs over them, or bucks them off. It's all the same to him, because eating grass or getting back with his buddies is way more important.

A horse handler who is in the habit of doing less than what it takes or quitting too soon teaches a horse that the human is nothing more than a big irritation to be ignored. When this happens, the horse can either become dull or dangerous. Nagging a horse teaches him to push on people or run right over the top of them. Remember, this horse views the person as an obstacle who is standing in the way between where he wants to go and what he desires. By never doing what it takes, a person teaches the horse that what he has to do to get rid of the irritation is up the ante. This can be very dangerous. Horses must know where the lines of acceptable behavior are because disrespectful behavior will degenerate over time. It will not get better until the horseman is willing to do something about it.

A case in point is a horse that shows aggression towards a person who enters a stall to feed him. It is not acceptable for a horse to harass the person by pushing into his space trying to snatch a bite of the food before it is placed in the container. This seemingly insignificant conflict can advance to more dangerous assaults such as biting, striking, or kicking. It is critical that the horseman defend their space in this type of confrontation by keeping the horse back. Otherwise someone may get hurt. It is vital that the horse learn to stand back and wait until the person gives him permission to eat.

The horse's attachment to a person who is too lenient will multiply one hundredfold if this person ever has the courage to be assertive enough to give the horse what he needs at the right time and in the proper amount. Until a person who lacks discipline has experienced this, it is very hard to convince them it will work. The main reason they don't believe it will work is they are afraid the horse will stop loving them if they do what is necessary. But the fact is the horse will not love them less, but *more*.

I believe we cannot project feelings of love onto a horse's emotions in the same way *we* experience love. Even though we can build a relationship of mutual respect, trust, and reliance with a horse, the deeper feelings of love are one-sided. They are not useful for modifying animal behavior. Please keep in mind that regardless of what lots of people think about this topic, I don't believe anyone really has a perfect or absolute idea of how horses experience emotions.

The core issue behind a person's inability to be firm and effective with a horse is that they are afraid of the horse. They are frustrated because the horse doesn't just do what they wish. Both the fear and frustration come from not being willing to find out how much reaction from the horse the person can take. Sooner or later an indulgent person will have to find out. If a horseman who is too easygoing doesn't learn how to do what it takes, they will end up getting hurt and killing their own dream. Although we don't have to fear horses, we should respect them as fellow creatures which are powerful animals whose actions can harm us if we are not careful. A person who is willing to do what it takes at the right time in the proper amount has the right attitude to win a horse's heart.

Doing More Than it Takes and Quitting Too Late

Now let's take a closer look at the other extreme, a horse handler who is way too strict. This person handles a horse without much, if any, thought on the process. They just want to get a job done, like ride from here to there and back without getting bucked off. It doesn't matter to this kind of rider whether the horse cares for the process or not, as long as he doesn't show his displeasure. The horse is also required to remain compliant at all times even when frightened. A horse who does not submit to these practices will find themselves at the sale barn in no time. Excuses run rampant, even to the point of blaming the horse's bad behavior on breeding rather than learning how to communicate and deal effectively with the horse's innate characteristics.

The reason a person may end up being too rough physically is they are out of mental and emotional control. They may even feel like the horse made them look bad in front of others. When a person becomes angry, adrenaline runs high, causing the body's motions to become jerky and way too forceful. The adrenaline rush interferes so much with the horseman's timing and *feel* that it causes total confusion for the horse. Even worse, their temper prevents them from knowing when to quit. A horseman who is too strict is not in the habit of allowing time to pause and reflect for either themselves or the horse. It is rare for an annoyed person to look back at themselves, resulting in difficulty identifying the true root of the problem. This type of horseman does not intend to set things up to teach the horse and make it easy for him to succeed. Too often their answer is punishment for misbehavior which most likely was a simple misunderstanding or fear. It is very easy to mix up firmness with punishment. They are never the same.

Why Punishment Doesn't Work

Punishment is the negative consequence of a particular action. Horses don't understand this because they need the consequence to happen when the horse starts to take action. In other words the pressure needs to be applied between thought and deed. Here is a simple illustration of why punishment does not work in the horse's mind. Let's say a horse breaks away from us and runs off. If we punish him in any way when we catch him he learns if you catch him, he will be punished. The next time we try to catch him it will be even more difficult to catch him. Is this what we wanted to teach the horse? Instead, when we catch him we must remain calm and pleasant no matter how angry we might be feeling. This takes a major act of self control. However, we must do it if we want to teach the horse that being caught is agreeable.

An electric fence is a perfect example of a simultaneous response to an action which is not punishment but rather a natural consequence to an action which modifies behavior immediately and permanently. It works because every time the animal touches the fence he gets shocked at that moment, no more, no less. It is not a judgmental consequence delivered in a way which causes resentment, disagreement, or a fight. I am not suggesting we put shock collars on our horses like I have heard of some people doing. Rather I am pointing out that the more consistent, fair, and immediate our response is to an action the more positive and lasting the desired changes will be.

Whenever a person trusts their strength or brute force, a common result is a confused, fearful, or angry horse. The horse handler who is too strict will have to let go of strength as a tool. Replacing it with the tool of understanding the mind of the horse will help the horseman learn to communicate in a way the horse understands. Clear communication with finesse will get better results than brute force. A horse handler who does more than it takes and quits too late cannot win a horse's heart even though the horse may seem obedient. A person who thinks the thousand pound animal beneath them is a thinking being which can and will respond with enthusiasm from very little effort on the part of the rider is on the correct path to winning a horse's heart.

The Self-Confident Attitude of Effective Leaders

Neither of the above described horse handlers are effective leaders or partners for any horse. An effective leader or partner is familiar with just how little or how much it takes to communicate clearly. This clarity will motivate each individual horse to perform to the best of his abilities. It is essential to know what to do, but it may be even more crucial to know when to quit. The most effective horse handler is a person with a positive mental attitude which is ingrained with clear, calm, and honest self confidence. A self-confident attitude is a key asset for every horseman to posses. Our attitudes, not our aptitude, are the chief determinant of our success. It is not to say we should throw out all our tools or quit learning techniques, because these are a necessary part of the journey. We should also be certain our attitudes compliment the tools and techniques we choose to use.

Attitudes are nothing more than habits of thought which determine actions. Habits can be acquired or changed. These changes come through internal understanding and acceptance. Humans are the only known creatures who can reshape themselves by altering their attitudes. We are either the masters or victims of our attitudes. It's a matter of personal choice where we can create our own destiny based on the mental emotional and physical habits we develop. We are where we are and what we are because of the thoughts that dominate our mind.

If we do not consciously form good habits while handling horses we will unconsciously form bad ones. Horses are quick to react out of instinct, but habits aren't the same as instincts. Habits don't just happen. They are caused. Once we determine the original cause of a habit we have the power to either accept or reject it and then change it or not.

Unconsciously forming a bad habit can be portrayed by a pattern I have seen many times when a person is attempting to put a horse in the trailer. I hear people say, "I can get my horse to go in the trailer, but he won't stay in." Before the person can shut the door or tie the horse up he turns around rushing out before anything can be done about it. When a horseman has this complaint about trailer loading I am almost positive the person has unintentionally formed this habit. The reason this happens is the person has created a pattern and horses are very good at learning patterns. A pattern can have both positive and negative effects like:

- The consistency of a pattern simplifies learning.
- Patterns can give a horse security.
- A pattern can help the horse anticipate the next action or movement.
- Too much repetition of a pattern can bore a horse so he acts up.
- Patterns by their very nature can produce either good or bad habits.

The troublesome habit of not staying in the trailer can be caused by a pattern the person allows to continue. Because a horseman has been taught to reward the slightest try by releasing the pressure, a horse handler often backs off the second the horse puts his front feet in the trailer. Sometimes this release allows the horse to relax so that he stands calmly with his front end in the trailer. He may or may not be thinking about getting in the trailer the rest of the way. But if he does get in the trailer all the way there is a fair chance he will stay in.

Another reaction to the release could be the horse quickly steps down backing out of the trailer. If this is his response to the release he is not thinking about getting in the trailer and most definitely is not thinking about staying in there if he does get in. There is nothing wrong with either of these responses. The problem starts when the handler permits the horse to immediately back out of the trailer turning into the person and leaving in a hurry. When this is done repeatedly the horseman has taught the horse an objectionable habit through using a pattern. It is very probable once the horse's whole body is in the trailer he may offer the same response when he feels the release, which is to turn and leave in a hurry. It shouldn't surprise the horse handler because the horse just did what he was taught to do.

I am not saying we shouldn't release the pressure on the slightest try or that we should force the horse in the trailer. I am saying we need to be careful how and where the horse moves after the release because everything we do matters. We need to examine what the release is teaching the horse. Our communication should be forming a habit that is advantageous to the horse and our relationship with him. If it is not, then we need to make the necessary adjustments so the feel we present to the horse forms beneficial habits which will help us get him in the trailer so he chooses to stay there.

Cultivating Positive Habits

Every person who is a successful horseman has formed the habit of doing things that failures dislike and will not do. They have good work habits which help develop an internal toughness. Their self-confident attitude will sustain them through every adversity and temporary discouragement they may face on the journey with their horse.

In order to become an excellent horseman we must cultivate good habits with a high purpose. Then we must be willing to change bad habits and attitudes for the better. It is difficult to let go of old habits and even more difficult to make permanent positive changes. If we resist change it will be the catalyst which crushes our dreams. If we embrace change we will find compelling motivation to create something new. This motivation can inspire enough courage to reach for our dreams no matter how elusive they may be.

The following are some negative habits and attitudes that we need to change in order to keep the dream alive:

- rushing
- making things too complicated
- tolerating unacceptable behaviors
- accepting mediocre results
- being too critical
- trying to make things happen
- doing things without enough preparation
- skipping foundational pieces
- relying on tools alone to solve problems
- not enough structure or focus
- too much anthropomorphism
- being too strict (aggressiveness)
- being too lenient (timidity)
- being too agenda driven

Good habits that we should cultivate are:

- taking the time it takes
- expect a lot but accept a little
- be particular not critical
- simplify things
- deal immediately with undesirable behaviors
- allow things to happen
- maintain foundation pieces
- observe & compare

There is more power in a positive progressive attitude than we have ever dreamed of. No matter what the level of our ability is we have more potential than we can ever develop in a lifetime. Just think about all the things people can do in this world. It is truly amazing. Some people can even do things with horses I never thought possible. The only limitations we have are those which are self-imposed.

Desire is the starting point for developing our potential. It is the precursor of things we are capable of doing, and weak desires produce weak results. The strength of genuine desire can take us through a difficulty which others will go around. The amount of desire we have is the inspiration which keeps the flame of progress burning within us. There are days we can look back with amazement at the strides we have made. Even with a great amount of progress it seems the more we know the more we realize there is still so much more to learn. When you have the courage to say to yourself, "I'm good, but not as good as I ought to be," then you have the right attitude which will win your horse's heart.

DOLLY: A New Beginning

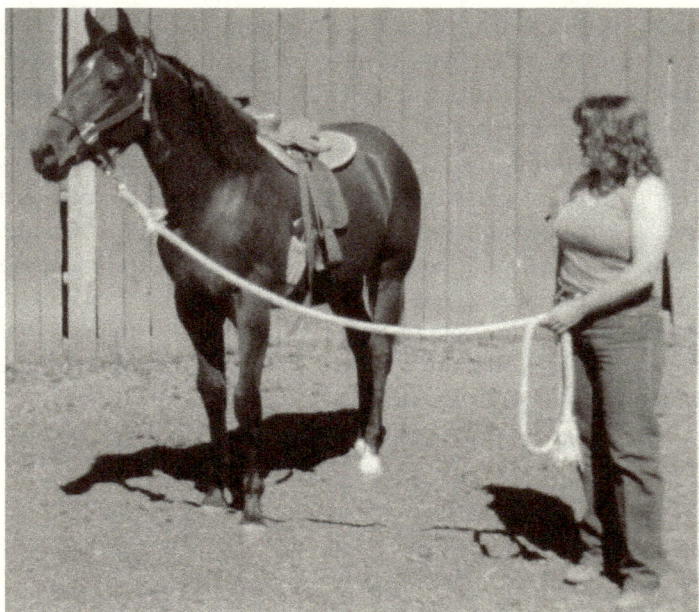

Dolly's first saddling

I don't believe it was just a coincidence Dolly was born one week before Slick died. She would be his replacement and the horse which would lead me on a brand new path. After Slick died on June 2nd, I couldn't even think about replacing him. When Keith and I were married in August of that same year my Dad gave Dolly to us for a wedding present. We would have to wait a couple more months until she was weaned before the bay filly with a white comma on her forehead could come home to live with us.

My Dad put her in the old two horse trailer he had bought in 1968. We met him in Torrington, WY in October. She stayed in the trailer while we watched my niece compete in the high school rodeo. We got back to Riverton well after midnight. Dolly had been in the trailer for two days. When we took her out she was so tired she could barely walk. She seemed to have drunk legs as we led her in the dark, half asleep, to her stall where Slick had lived only six months earlier.

As Dolly grew I began to read some books on horse training because I decided I was going to start this horse the right way. After Slick I had to admit I didn't know quite as much about horses as I thought I did. I didn't want to make the same mistakes I had made in the past. And so began a new phase in my horsemanship journey. I had a new horse with a clean slate. If she didn't turn out well I had no one to blame except myself.

Things were different now because I had a much better attitude about horsemanship. My goals had changed from focusing on me and what pleasure or recognition I received from a horse, to focusing on the horse and what I could do for them as a partner and leader. However, I was still lacking some essential techniques which matched my new improved attitude.

In January during a turn-out session Dolly slipped on the ice while playing in her typical exuberant fashion. She broke her right hind leg. After the initial panic that I might have to put her down just six months after loosing Slick, I relaxed when the x-rays showed it was only a cracked growth plate. The veterinarian said she would heal well. However, it meant stall rest and lots of daily treatments. I bonded with this little filly during this period and developed an even deeper devotion to do things right this time around.

The following spring when Dolly was a yearling Keith and I

bought two other horses for riding. Shortly after they arrived Dolly jumped a six foot panel trying to get back in with the new horses. She made it to the other side but her legs were caught and she was lying upside down. Thankfully, Keith and I saw it happened. Keith was able to relax her by holding her head down, petting and talking to her, while I untangled her legs. We rolled her over and she got up. I was so afraid of what the damages might be when she stood up and took a step. After shaking it off, she walked away like nothing happened. My heart attack was over and I wondered how I was every going to survive the journey with this horse. Didn't she know I had a new attitude with her best interest in my heart? Why did she have to keep making my commitment so difficult?

Dolly recovering from her leg fracture

I started doing some ground work with Dolly that summer. My skills to apply the techniques I read in books were crude at best. However, it was still a great improvement from my past mentality of "saddlem'up and ride". Never mind about whether it is good for the horse or not. All you have to do is hold on and ride'm even if they are scared or don't understand. Right?

I spent more time preparing Dolly to ride than any previous horse and it paid off. By the time she was two I had attended my first horsemanship clinic. I was so anxious to ride her so I could use the new knowledge and skills I was learning. My first rides on her were quite uneventful, unlike most of my other attempts at starting a colt, which were more like a dust storm. It was a wonderful new beginning. I didn't know it would be so much easier and safer when one has some good techniques coupled with understanding about the horse's perspective and a better attitude.

I showed Dolly in both English and Western when she was two, three, and four years old and she did very well. We were off to a great start, or so I thought. I was pretty proud and had no idea I would soon get knocked down a few notches. It seems every time I start thinking I am better then I really am, life comes at me hard and I have to get off my high horse. Sometimes the fall is painful.

As Dolly grew so did my knowledge of ways which are better for the horse. I wish I could say I made no mistakes with her. She taught me I was still a long way from the perfect horseman I wanted to be. Even though I am still striving for perfection, or maybe I should say excellence, I am now able to admit my mistakes, give myself permission to experiment, and seek creative ways to solve problems when they arise.

One of the biggest mistakes I made with Dolly was at a clinic when she was five years old. This clinic brought another new beginning in my life. She is the first horse I was injured on seriously enough to require surgery. Oh I had bumps and bruises along the way, but nothing like this. All of the previous accidents I had with horses were due to my ignorance and inept abilities to read the horse and respond properly. But this time I could not plead ignorance because I knew better. I deserved the blame for my injury because I did not follow the truth of the principles I had been learning the last few years. Call it a lapse in judgment. It was the final blow to my ego which taught me that savvy horsemen know the heart of a horse and how to win it.

Competing on Dolly as a three year old

I was participating in a clinic where the instructor asked us to line up stirrup to stirrup with only a couple of feet in-between the horses. We were told to ride our horse in a serpentine between the other horses. They explained the purpose of this exercise was to help the horses improve social behavior in a crowded riding environment.

Dolly went through the first two slots just fine. Then when we approached the third one, where she was face to face with a horse which had kicked her earlier, she refused to go. I was told to force her forward with spurs. She refused again by going backwards in a hurry. This was the first visible sign of high tension which I noticed. I'm sure she had been trying to communicate to me her lack of confidence in this situation before this, but I wasn't listening. I forged ahead anyway, going against Dolly's sense of self-preservation.

The clinician and his assistant continued to tell me to put more energy into making her go through this tight squeeze. The next sign which told me she was becoming even more distressed was rearing. But I refused to listen and kept forcing her through her threshold digging the spurs into her sides without consideration. The tension began to build stronger and stronger. I could feel her tail getting tighter and tighter. The hump developing in her back was unmistakable. She pinned her ears all the way down. At this point I should have listened to my horse and quit listening to the orders to keep doing what wasn't working. I should have respected my horse's deep sense of self-preservation.

Some of the things I should have done include:

1. Open up the hole by separating the horses a little more so she didn't feel so trapped.
2. Disengage the hindquarters to loosen her up, instead of forcing her straight forward.
3. Applied the approach and retreat principle.
4. Circled in from behind or around the horses, instead of trying the same head-on path.
5. Ride back and forth in front of the horses until she felt more confident.

6. Use a string for spanking on the butt to create energy,
    instead of spurring in the belly.
7. We could have tried another slot with a familiar horse
    or ones which were friendlier.
8. I should have slowed down, taking the attitude, if
    this takes two days, that's ok.
9. It may have helped to get off and send her through on
    the ground first.
10. We could have asked all the horses to start moving,
    so we could weave in and out of them. This would
    have encouraged her to move more freely and not be
    so frightened.

All of these ideas would have set her up for success by
building her confidence. They may have allowed her to think
this wasn't such a bad idea because her self-preservation
wasn't at stake. When I suggested these ideas, I was advised,
"Yes, we could have opened up the hole and made it easier
for her. We could have let her think it was her idea. But we
needed to get across to her that we were in charge, it was
our idea, and she needed to comply with our idea no matter
what." This advice may have its place in certain situations
when a horse is confident. Although through this experience
and many others I have learned whenever a horse is tight and
scared in self-preservation mode, if we physically force them
into a situation with no thought of their mental condition we
shouldn't be surprised when they explode like a bomb. That
is exactly what happened.

When Dolly exploded she was finished with warnings.
Because of her natural instinct of self-preservation she simply
hit the eject button. I'm sure she felt she had only one way
left to escape the extreme pressure I continued to hammer
her with. I have never felt a more violent buck. She did not
go forward as in a normal buck. Instead she went straight up

and down, landing in the same tracks each time, until she launched me. I landed on my shoulder, tearing my rotator cuff, bicep and triceps.

I do not blame the clinician, his assistant, or Dolly for these injuries. I blame myself because I went against so many of the principles which I believe in. I did this in the face of peer pressure. I didn't want to be different. I thought I had to do what I was being told. I should have said, "No, thanks, we'll sit this one out for now. Maybe we'll try this some other day!" But I continued when I knew better. It was a mistake I hope I never make again. I learned two very important lessons that day: Trust my own instincts no matter what anyone else says! And stick to a set of tried and true principles, even if I look silly to others. Just before Dolly blew I was thinking, "There has to be a better way... What if...?" By then it was too late.

I hope by reading my story you will learn from my mistake. Be strong to be who you are and refuse to do anything which doesn't line up with your principles and values, no matter who is asking you to do it. You know your own limitations and those of your horse better than anyone else. Don't be afraid to say no or just get off when you know you are way beyond your capabilities.

But, there is a fine line between knowing your limitations and letting your fears override your progression. Learn to know and recognize the difference, because this is an individual decision based on your own skills and experience. All you can do is make a true effort to be the best you can be and then rely on yourself. Let experience determine your evolution. The most valuable learning experiences aren't always positive ones.

As a result of this incident, I have a deeper awareness of the importance of true horsemanship through feel, its concepts and principles. This accident gave me a stronger confidence in myself both as a horseman and as a teacher. I've come out of this a better person. I now recognize the ability of a horse to give us appropriate feedback in every situation. I also realized how essential it is to listen to the feedback a horse is giving us, then finding a way to deal with it in a manner the horse understands and can appreciate.

Sherry on Dolly with Keith on Cisco the 2nd day after Dolly ejected Sherry.

After I wiped the dust off, all I can remember is there was some cowboy riding Dolly on a dead run up and down the arena doing sliding stops as I passed out in the grand stands. I didn't ride the rest of the day and wondered how poor Dolly was doing. Despite the pain, the next day Keith boosted me up on Dolly with my arm in a homemade tea towel sling. I had never been this scared on a horse. Up until this point in my life I had been a pretty fearless rider. However, that morning the first canter departure in the correct lead left my heart in the pit of my stomach. After completing a flying lead change I cried because I knew I could still do it. The tears were also for Dolly who I knew would take care of me, if I would take care of her. I did not win her heart that day, but she had won mine! It was a milestone for me.

I completed the rest of the clinic riding with one arm, being more careful to listen to my horse's feedback. By the end of the day I overcame my fear and I had a better understanding of how to relate to others with fears. The best advice I have for someone with fears is: Take a step to conquer your fears as I did. Don't let fears paralyze you. Get knowledge and use wisdom at all times when you are in the presence of horses. Don't take unnecessary risks, but push yourself a little. Otherwise you won't ever get out of your comfort zone. If you don't ever get out of your comfort zone you won't overcome your fears. Horses are fun, with dangers that can be minimized if we are able to determine when we have reached an impassable limit of either the horse or the human.

Someone told me "as time passes you will come to a clearer understanding of these events." I believe that is true. As I reflect on this story I see it caused a setback in my relationship with Dolly. Rebuilding was sometimes hard.

Dolly didn't trust me as much, and I didn't blame her. I had withdrawn a huge sum from our relationship account that day. She had tried to tell me how she was feeling with polite responses at first. But when that didn't work she resorted to more vigorous responses until she finally let me know in no uncertain terms I was pressing too hard. I hope to never lose the smart bumps I got from this. I am reminded of this humiliating experience every time I lift my right arm and feel the twinge of pain, remembering I have lost some range of motion.

It's a good thing horses are so forgiving because Dolly has never retaliated like that since. This is proof to me that horses don't seek revenge and they do forgive. Maybe they don't forget, but I think they do forgive. I have learned to forgive myself for making the mistakes I made with Dolly. Remember I wanted to do things the right way with her because she was a new beginning for me. Even though I had a head full of new knowledge and a bigger pocketful of skills and techniques, I still made mistakes with Dolly. She was supposed to be my perfect clean slate. I had dirtied the slate and even put some scratches in it. We both survived the wounds and haven't been afraid to start over. Dolly showed me my imperfections. She taught me that in order to win a horse's heart tools and techniques alone are not enough. They must be used with the proper attitude and a person who is willing to listen to feedback.

The good news is Dolly has turned out to be a really nice riding horse even with all my blunders. I use her for lessons with people who need more confidence. She still amazes me at what she will do for them and for me despite my mistakes with her. We enjoy a lot of beautiful rides together. I feel elegant and important when I'm on her back. But I'm still not sure I have won her heart all the way, because sometimes she seems aloof and far off even though she is being obedient. If I stay true to sound principles, good judgment, and listen to her feedback I know one day I will win her heart. Then we'll be elegant together.

Sherry riding Dolly bareback at one of her Women's Confident
Leadership Camps
(Photographer Jessica McCaslin, Custer County Chief)

Chapter 6: Fears vs. Confidence

"Let me tell you the secret that has led me to my goal. My strength lies solely in my tenacity." -- Louis Pasteur

As I travel, the statement I hear more than any other is, "I want more confidence with my horse." Almost everyone has experienced some kind of fear when dealing with a horse. Certain people are overcome with fear and others hide it quite well. Either way, at some point in our horsemanship journey we will experience some form of fear, which means we may need a boost of confidence in order to keep progressing forward to our dreams.

Some of the fears I hear people express which hold them back from living their dream are:
- Fear of letting go of old beliefs and having to admit they were wrong
- Fear the new methodologies we are learning might not work with all horses
- Fear we might misinterpret what we have been taught
- Fear we might mess up or worse yet ruin our horse
- Fear we might teach the horse the wrong or bad things
- Fear we can't trust our own instincts, knowledge, skills, and tools

- Fear we might not listen to the horse
- Fear we can't read the horse well enough to interpret the feedback and thus use the right technique
- Fear we might get hurt or even hurt the horse
- Fear of working with the horse alone with no supervision
- Fear the horse might not like us
- Fear others might not like us if we are better than them
- Fear we won't learn fast enough to keep up with others
- Fear we might look stupid or foolish
- Fear we might look proud, egotistical, or snobbish
- Fear we might not be able to meet our responsibilities with home, family and job if we get in a wreck

Notice all of these fears are based on what might happen. Don't think about the things that might happen or the things you can't do. Rather focus on the things you can do.

Conquering Fear

"The key to success is for you to make a habit throughout your life of doing the things you fear." -- Vincent Van Gogh

Dig to the Root Causes of Fear

When we think about very specific fears related to riding a horse they include:

1. Fear of loss of balance and falling off thus getting injured.

2. Fear of insufficient skill or knowledge about how to read a horse and therefore what to do about unsafe behaviors such as kicking, biting, pulling back, bucking, rearing, spooking, etc.
3. Fear of the unknown (the things we haven't done yet with a horse but want to) like a first ride, cantering, trail riding, winning a competition, etc.

Most of the time, fears are caused by an unresolved incident from the past. An accident with a horse, or a serious injury resulting from handling them, can keep a person from stepping up and conquering fears. This seems to be justifiable. However, sometimes after a bad experience a person spends way too much time mulling over what they did wrong. By doing this they succeed in scaring themselves way more than the accident or injury warranted. Some fears are actually wisdom because they keep you from real danger. This kind of fear should not be ignored. Being able to discern the difference between real and perceived danger can help a person begin to deal with fears in a constructive way.

I have discovered those with the most paralyzing fear have never had a serious accident or injury with a horse. At first this was puzzling to me. As I examined the roots of human fears I found fear is often connected to the perception of losing something. A person can be afraid of losing many things like: face, love, control, confidence, respect, health, money, friendship, or even life. People with paralyzing fear also seem to have another thing in common: Low self esteem. A low self image forms an invisible ceiling which stops a person from attempting to rise or progress above self-imposed limitations. It is almost impossible to do anything in a positive way while holding negative feelings about self.

A person paralyzed by fear rarely does anything with their horse beyond providing physical care. Others are ok handling their horse from the ground but the minute they think about being above the horse they get queasy. These people need our empathy and compassion because they already feel guilt and hate the whipped feeling they have when they fail to get on their horse.

The reason people end up with debilitating fear is they let the fear grow in their mind. When they do this their brain goes into survival mode, which causes the person to find ways to avoid doing anything with their horse. This person is better at talking themselves out of doing something than talking themselves into doing something with their horse, especially if it is something new. They tend to just do over and over that which they are already comfortable doing. The pattern of doing the same thing will just dig a deeper rut. If a person never moves out of their comfort zone they will not move closer to their dream or have the courage to win a horse's heart.

We all know trying to muster up enough power to push through a fear to make it go away just doesn't work. Ignoring it doesn't work any better. So what does work? Take a deep breath and try saying something like this, "Yikes, I'm afraid right now, so let me see what I can do at this point to move forward a little bit." Then ask, "What small step can I take to move a little closer to my dream?" Next take a baby step, no matter how small it is. Remember, a small step is better than no step at all. Progress does not have to be fast or giant. Don't expect too much too soon. Keep taking one step at a time and before you know it you will wonder what all the fuss was about. Celebrate the slightest try of each baby step, even if to others the progress may not look like much effort. It, in fact, may be a monumental performance.

Practical Steps to Help us Overcome Fears

1.   Try Forgiveness:
There can be a lot of guilt tied to fears. Sometimes the pain is almost intolerable until we forgive ourselves for the mistakes we've made. As soon as we forgive ourselves for the stupid mistakes we made and quit living in the past we are able to quit worrying about making the same mistake in the future. Forgiveness will set us free to move forward with confidence and leave behind the fear.

2.   Use Affirmations:
The power of thoughts and words cannot be overlooked. A person with high fear and low self esteem must change their thinking and choose with wisdom the words they speak. It's a good idea to start with some self talk. You might say something like this: "I am good enough, brave enough, fierce enough, and determined enough, to handle my horse with savvy. I have the correct knowledge, tools, and strategies to ride my horse with confidence." We need to take charge of our thinking, choices, and our words. There are no expectations placed upon us to perform except those we place on ourselves.

3.   Concentrate on the relationship:
It is very effective to build a better relationship with a horse through ground activities. I often hear comments like this about ground work: "I'm not good at it." "I don't like it." "I don't see the point." "That's just a waste of time, I would rather ride." While all these comments are real to the person, the fact remains the better communication one has with a horse on the ground the more confident both will be when it comes to riding. Every wise horseman knows if you want to

be good with horses, being able to sit a saddle well is not enough. You must also have good ground handling skills to be the very best. Remember the purpose of working with a horse on the ground is to develop and improve the relationship. The riding experience will become less stressful when we are confident about the relationship we have developed with the horse through ground activities. We will be better equipped to conquer any fears related to riding when we have put in the time and effort to improve our ground handling skills. If we want a nice riding experience it is advantageous to be careful what we teach a horse when we are not riding him because everything we do on the ground with a horse will transfer to the saddle.

4. **Start Momentum:**
In the book "Move Closer Stay Longer" by Stephanie Burns she suggests the ten minute rule where you pick something to do with a horse and stick with it for ten minutes. She says that if a person can do this they will get hooked and the momentum will carry them through to do more. This is a very simple and yet powerful strategy for overcoming fears. Be willing to confront obstacles and situations even for just a second, and then a minute or two building up the momentum. Each experience will take you closer to first controlling the fear and eventually eliminating it. Progression is the key. Don't try to get on the horse and go for a twenty mile trail ride the first day. The starting point is determined by how out of control the fear has become. Try doing each of the following activities for ten minutes until it feels comfortable to move on to the next. If it takes a day, a month, or years, ten minutes at a time, it doesn't matter. Getting the momentum started is what is important.

Here are some simple suggestions to get you started. There are other creative ideas you can do just use your imagination.

- Sit in the house and visualize the dream
- Watch the horse from the window
- Pet the horse from the other side of the fence
- Sit on the fence and watch the horse
- Catch and Halter the horse
- Brush the horse
- Put the saddle pad on the horse
- Saddle the horse
- Take the horse for a walk in the corral or arena
- Do ground activities with the horse
- Learn to do great lateral flexion
- Lead the horse on a trail walk
- Sit on the fence with the horse saddled, pet him all over
- Put your foot in the stirrup
- Swing your leg over and then dismount right away
- Sit on the horse; if needed let someone hold the lead rope
- Sit on the horse doing lateral flexion
- Ride the horse one step; if needed use someone next to the horse
- Build from there. You get the idea!

I recommend Stephanie's book for further reading on this subject.

5. Stick with a program:
Often we have fears because we haven't worked at something long enough to see it succeed. We give up too soon. If you don't know what ground activities to do in order to develop a better relationship as suggested above, find a program or instructor who can help you. There are

a ton of programs on the market to choose from. With the flood of DVD's, books, tapes, clinicians, horse TV, blogs, chat groups, study groups, and home study courses for sale, there is no excuse today for not knowing what to do. Although some of this information isn't cheap, the alternative is much more expensive.

A wise person is a person who knows what they don't know and are not afraid to admit it. Whether it's raising children, learning to play an instrument, participate in a sport, or training a horse, a program with objectives and a concrete plan will give us more confidence in our ability to get the job done. More confidence equals less fear. I am not going to endorse or tear apart any one program. However, I do recommend picking one and sticking with it for at least two years before you start mixing things up. This will provide a consistency of progression which will provide security. Security is a good thing for someone trying to overcome fear. Even though it will be tempting to skip parts or jump around, it is best to stick with one program as written long enough to see it work.

6. **Safety by Reading the Horse:**
    By learning how to accurately read a horse we will know what to do with the feedback the horse gives us. This will take away a lot of uncertainty by itself. Fear of the unknown isn't staring us in the face if we learn how to read a horse and deal with his feedback in a positive manner. I hear so many people say, "When I was a kid I rode without any fear, but now everything scares me to death." My story is a little different. When I was a kid I rode without fear most of the time. However, I also rode some very rank young horses. I had good reason to be afraid of some of them. I got on these horses even when I was afraid because I trusted my Dad's judgment.

If he thought I could do it then I better get the job done. I have less fear now than I have ever had in my life, because I have the knowledge about how to deal with situations as they arise. Even more important, I have learned how to read a horse, which can prevent many undesirable problems. I am much safer now because I follow a foundational program which prepares the horse for success.

Being safe is a key element in controlling fear. Being able to read a horse can help keep us safe. Know the difference between real danger and perceived danger triggered by your irrational fears. When real danger is involved, stop. Just quit, and save your life. Don't worry about who wins. You won't be able to win your horses heart if you are injured or dead. Safety first!

Dealing with the Horse's Fear

Before I move to the topic of confident leadership it is important we mention the horse's fear. This topic could take up an entire book by itself because horses have been known to be afraid of clippers, needles, syringes, paste wormer, farriers, vets, and trailers. Some horses are scared to death of other animals like: pigs, sheep, goats, cows, buffalo, deer, elk, rabbits, squirrels, birds, dogs, and cats. Don't forget that many horses dread anything to do with water, center pivots, sprinklers, bridges and ditches. It seems very silly to us that gates, doors, signs, mailboxes, tin cans, tires, and yellow lines on the highway, can horrify a horse. Anyone who has been trail riding has discovered that UPS trucks, motorcycles, bicycles, hikers, very small children, and drunks can cause a horse to panic. Then there are the terrorizing bushes, trees, poop piles, shadows , and lumps of dirt.. Plus we must never underestimate the dread of sounds like: guns, fireworks, loud speakers, horns, and whistles. And finally simple thing like: ropes, whips, plastic bags, blue tarps, card board, flags, and balloons, can alarm the best horse unexpectedly. We all know this list is certainly incomplete. There are avid trail riders who can more than double this list.

Some people go out of their way to make sure their horse doesn't get afraid. We hear them saying things like "Don't do that. It might scare my horse," or "Please put that away. My horse is afraid of it." The main thing to avoid is letting your horse train you to avoid these things. Learn how to educate your horse and expose him to as many things as you can so he can learn to handle his fears in a safer way.

Some horses are afraid of their own shadow. This horse needs a confident, sensitive, fair leader at all times This type of horse is usually very sensitive and so unconfident they are always on the edge of self preservation. They are misunderstood by many people who think they are stupid or crazy. When a human is either fearful or overbearing around this type of horse the problems are compounded.. When the human spooks, the horse may think, "Oh no, it even scared the person. We better get the heck outta'here!"

On the opposite end of the scale there are horses which are quite brave and confident. These horses have a tendency to be on the dull side and are often labeled stubborn or lazy. When a human is fearful around this horse, the horse usually takes over, pushing the person around, doing as he pleases. This horse also needs a confident leader who isn't afraid to be assertive enough in order to motivate the horse to become a respectful partner. However, a person who tries to force this horse by pure physical power can cause the horse to become even duller. Worse yet, the result may end up in a fight where nobody wins. In order to motivate this kind of horse a horseman may have to resort to unconventional ideas. Find out what makes this horse tick then provide the appropriate rewards for motivation instead of thinking punishment. But remember, don't let him bully you, which is what the fearful person often allows.

It is impossible to fool a horse by faking it. So in order to help a horse deal with his fears we must deal with our own first. After we have learned to control our own fear we are prepared to help a horse overcome his fears. The best way to do this is the same way we conquered our own. They key principle taught by many popular clinicians is approach and retreat. The retreat is so critical because being able to move away from the scary object is what convinces the horse he is not going to die. The approach gives the horse the opportunity to investigate and process whatever he is afraid of until he becomes curious. When the horse becomes curious he is well on his way to controlling his fear.

We should not expect a horse to never be afraid again any more than we can expect that of ourselves. But what we can do is help the horse learn self-control when faced with something he perceives as dangerous. The most important strategy we can teach the horse is to turn, face, wait and think, instead of snort, fart and bolt before figuring out what it is he is afraid of. The worst thing we can do is block the horse by pulling back on two reins. This will add claustrophobia to an already out of control situation. If the rider blocks the horse in this way more often than not the horse ends up rearing. The safe answer is to disengage the horse's hindquarter with one rein. Next allow the horse to turn, face, and wait for a moment while assessing the situation. Then move the horse on as quickly as possible. Don't sit around waiting for more to happen. Give the horse something to do so he can think about something else. Or better yet, assess the situation *before* it gets to this out of control point. Prevention is always a better option. This takes a powerful focus on the part of a rider. A consistent connection with a horse takes a lot of patience and practice. The bonus is being able to put a stop to accidents caused by fear before they happen.

The Emergency Stop

The one rein emergency stop is the technique taught and stressed by almost every popular clinician. If you don't know how to do it, it is time to learn. I recommend you do more than just learn it. I recommend you become so good at it that it is instinctual for both you and your horse. I have heard people say, "This technique isn't all it's cracked up to be and you can pull a horse over." They are correct, because if you don't do your homework, then it is your own fault if it doesn't work. If you don't do it right it is possible to pull a horse over. So get it right, because someday your life might depend on it. Consider it your emergency brake. I've never had it fail me yet. I once heard a very popular clinician say something like this, "If I could teach every horse owner in America just one technique, it would be the one rein stop."

Not too long ago I was riding Dolly out in the hills. We were heading back home a different route than usual. We had been cantering circles around cedar trees. I was giving her a break to cool down. As we were walking along she tensed up, hesitating to go forward. I looked around and didn't see anything, so I encouraged her to walk on. She hadn't taken more than a dozen steps when about six grouse flew up right in front of us. She jumped less than I did. The amazing thing was she did *not* follow her natural instinct to run off. Even though her feet got happy for a second, she remembered right away the smart and safe thing to do was turn, face, and wait. She did a one-rein stop by herself before I had time to take control. This is what I mean by practicing it until it becomes instinctual. We can't prevent horses from startling at objects like birds flying up in front of them any more than I can stop myself from spooking at a rattlesnake. But what we can do is help a horse learn to spook in place and control their reactions to fear.

Using one rein to stop does not produce an immediate stop. Rather it is changing the direction of the feet by winding down in a circular fashion. It is a gradual slowing down of the feet so we can dismount with safety. If we don't train for it we will have problems when we need it in an emergency situation.

Knowing you can stop your horse in an emergency situation with one rein will give you a peace of mind which will calm your fears. The one rein stop is not only the emergency brake which can keep you safe, it is a training tool used to increase accuracy, balance, and control for both the horse and rider. Practicing it will help improve both physical and mental performance no matter what activity one chooses to participate in with a horse. It is a powerful technique when practiced and used correctly because it redirects the energy of the horse when he has lost self-control. When a horse has lost control he is often in self-preservation mode. This can be dangerous because the horse has quit thinking with the left side of his brain.

The reasons slowing the horse down with one rein works so well is: As soon as the horse turns and disengages his hindquarters his left-brain mode of thinking returns so he can decide what to do next. This is something a horse will do naturally when humans are not involved. It is called flight distance, which is the distance a wild horse runs before he turns to look back at a predator chasing him. It is approximately 440 yards. A bit further than a lion can run at full speed. He runs out of juice after about four hundred yards. I'm not suggesting that it will take 440 yards to stop a horse with one rein, but it will take mental stamina to outlast the horse's determination. I have found that most people have about a thirty second threshold before they will give up on something and say, "This doesn't work." For the one rein stop to work well a horseman has to get a better handle on their own attention span, developing more personal discipline as it relates to consistency. A horseman must be willing to take the time it takes to get the one rein stop right before he needs to use it to save his life.

Emotional and Mental Control Precede Physical Control

So many times in our enthusiasm to perform we go straight to the physical and ignore the emotional and mental issues. Remember emotional and mental control precede physical control, not the other way around. Most people think that if they get physical control of the horse they will get emotional and mental control, but this isn't always true. Interrupting a negative behavior pattern will give the horse something else to think about. Then his body reactions can change. When we learn to deal with the emotional and mental side of the horse first, the consequence is often the disappearance of harmful physical symptoms.

Any effective communication begins with having the listener's attention. When working with horses I have found many of them are not in the habit of giving their attention to a human. I believe this is often the cause of a lot of the difficulties people experience with their horse. Being able to gain and hold a horse's attention is the first step in getting physical control of a horse. I have been pondering why so many of us tend to skip this first step. Perhaps it is so basic and such a subtle step that we take it for granted. Since it is so important for the safety of the human and dealing with the horse's fears I think it is worth giving some thought and consideration to this seldom-discussed.

We need to have the learner's attention when we explain a task if we expect our directions to be followed. Since I am a retired school teacher and many of you reading this may have children I can make the analogy of teaching children. For example, if we want to help a child learn a math concept or the meaning of a word, but they are staring out the window watching other kids play on the playground, they won't learn a thing until we get their attention. It is no different with horses, except that we may also have fears to deal with.

Every good horseman is aware at least subconsciously all the time of making sure he has the horse's attention before attempting to elicit a response. They achieve this by doing just enough to warrant the horse's attention. It could be something as simple as a shift of weight, a flick of a finger, a gentle tap on the withers, a soft bump on the lead rope, or a change in expression of the handler to distract the horse from whatever he is focusing on back to the handler. The key is to stop doing whatever we did to get the horse's attention the moment we get it. Consistency will pay off. , The sooner we repeat the process when the horse's attention wanders again, the less we will have to do to get his focus back. If we can do this without being over demanding and at the same time arouse the horse's curiosity, then the horse will start to stay with us mentally longer and longer. It takes a person who is acutely aware of when the horse's attention is about to leave in order to make cues more and more subtle until they are nearly invisible to the untrained eye.

We can tell if a horse's mind is on the handler by checking to see if his eyes or ears are towards the person. If the horse's head goes up and he looks off in another direction to watch what is happening somewhere else then the handler needs to bring his attention back before trying to ask the horse to do something. If the horse is just being curious then we might just wait a minute for the horse to come back with us. However, when the horse is afraid, we need to get his attention back for safety reasons. Because when a frightened horse's attention leaves that is the moment we begin to lose influence over the situation. First his mind goes and then his feet, followed by ribs and hips. The person on the end of the lead had better watch out if he is in the fearful horse's tracks. If we will develop the habit of tipping a horse's mind back towards us early and as often as necessary, we can avoid a lot of accidents and phrases like "he didn't even warn me", or "I don't know what happened, he just..."

It is important to learn to read the indicators which tell us the horse's thoughts are going elsewhere. Some of these include: Body tension, drifting a certain direction, ears and head coming up, and the direction he is looking. When immediate danger is apparent it is better to keep control over the situation before a horse is too far gone mentally and emotionally. By being aware, reading the signs and keeping the horse connected to you a lot of unsafe situations can be avoided. We can try tipping the horse's nose for a step or two at the first sign of discomfort, thus redirecting his mind back to our ideas. Before we can be heard by a horse we have to get his attention. Then he can follow our directions.

It is the habits we develop in a controlled environment that will either ensure or impair our success of keeping a horse with us mentally and then physically when we are in an unfamiliar or threatening situation. If we are in the habit of letting a horse's mind wander, tuning us out, then we shouldn't be surprised when his concerns take him someplace other than where we want him to go.

We must first be able to gain and hold our own attention, before we can expect a horse to do the same. This may take practice. It is not a habit that comes easy to some horsemen. When gaining and holding our own attention becomes second nature to us we will be able to subconsciously keep track of the horse's attention. Consistently giving our attention to the horse is the start of gaining and holding his attention. Protecting and keeping the horse's mental and emotional concentration will give us more physical control over the horse's fears and actions.

My experience has proven to me it is a lot easier to get horses over their fears than it is some humans. Maybe horses have more HORSE SENSE than we do. Most horses are much more adaptable to change than many humans are. Being gregarious is part of a horse's temperament. Therefore they are natural followers. If we can convince a horse we are a worthy leader who knows what he is doing he'll follow us anywhere and do anything for us. A horse will not give his heart over 100% to a fearful person because they are only looking for confident leaders to follow who can gain and hold their attention.

Confident Leadership

"The man who has confidence in himself gains the confidence of others." -- Hasidic saying

Command of Horses Begins with Command of Self

Confidence can be described as a feeling, a state of mind, and the lack of fear or self doubt. A person who is confident knows they have the knowledge, ability, and desire to "Get'r done." We understand how powerful confidence can be yet how elusive the feeling can be. Confidence or the lack thereof, affects our goals, motivation, relationships, and our self-image. Our self-image affects our ability to be a leader. Because a horse is looking for confident leadership our ability to lead affects our performance.

Successful leaders have a positive, progressive attitude which we have already discussed in chapter five. They recognize the creative potential of everyone on their team and have the ability to make productive use of it. The best leaders have good work habits including time management skills. Self-direction is also an important quality and the most effective leaders lead by example, not by edict.

Superior leaders are not restricted by the way things have always been done. They continually search for the best way, not just the most familiar ways to get things done. The distinguishing mark of a true leader is the ability to make decisions. Command of others, especially a horse, begins with command of oneself. The ability to influence a horse starts with knowing where we stand and where we are going. Without this knowledge, self confidence is a fleeting thing which becomes situational depending on the environment or circumstances.

Whether confidence is being built up or torn down depends on how a person perceives things at any given moment. The more we know about any given situation and what to do about it the more confident we will be. Self-confidence can be gained only through practical know how. Know how comes from knowledge and experience. Experience can only be gleaned through a willingness to move out of our comfort zone. In other words knowledge, experience, and success breed confidence.

Confidence is demonstrated by action. With a clear vision and strong desire to take a first step we can get so busy taking action we won't have time to be afraid anymore. This will reinforce the ability we have to get the job done. This ability can give us the strength needed to sweep away all obstacles. When obstacles disappear our strength is renewed and our energy is rejuvenated. If we use some of this extra energy to expand mental thinking it will enhance decision making. Sound decisions can improve overall performance. Improvement equals success and success leads to even more confidence.

Although confidence is demonstrated by action, actions are a choice. There are certain choices we can make which will ensure confidence building and other choices will destroy it. Here are some suggestions of choices we can make which will lead to more confidence.

Choices Which Build More Confidence

1. **Choose time and preparation**
    One of the best guarantees for more confidence is prior and proper preparation. This requires self-discipline with patience in order to slow down and take the time it takes. It is important to practice with progression, purpose, and concentration. Just going through the motions won't get the desired results. There is no doubt that skipping key elements in training can ruin the confidence of both the horse and rider. Learn how to manage time and stick with a program as suggested in the previous chapter. Plenty of time and preparation will help build confidence.

2. **Choose realistic expectations with consistency**
    Don't expect perfection all the time or overnight because this leads to frustration and discouragement.

Discouragement can make one give up. Instead of perfection, strive for consistency. Keep expectations realistic and only increase them as skill level improves. Slow and calculated progression with consistency will provide successful accomplishment of small tasks which will build confidence faster than trying to achieve perfection in a hurry.

3. Choose to learn from mistakes
Mistakes are part of every journey. Choose to view a mistake as a temporary setback. If we hang on to mistakes or make excuses for them we lose the opportunity to learn from them. Learning from our mistakes means we are able to deal honestly with our shortcomings and compels us to make consistent corrections. These significant changes for the better will lead to even more confidence.

4. Choose optimism and manage emotional fitness
Believe you will be successful. Use positive affirmations when faced with new challenges or dealing with plateaus that seem to never end. Don't forget to look back at the progress you've made. Stop listening to that little voice of doubt which is a reminder of all of the mistakes you've made. This little voice will keep bringing up all the things which could possible go wrong in the future unless you turn it off. If you listen to this negative voice it will chip away at self-esteem, causing you to question your abilities and eventually paralyzing you from moving forward. Fight back, take action, and start talking back with positive affirmations every time it speaks.

5. Choose an instructor, plus share, and receive feedback
If we surround ourselves with uplifting and inspiring people in a positive environment it will boost our

confidence level. Be careful who you hang out with.
When I was a kid my dad always told me if you want to
fly with the eagles don't hang out with chickens. Spend
time with others who have been there and have risen
above their own fears. This will provide invaluable
feedback for continued growth and learning. Find
an instructor, a riding buddy, or study group where
sharing and receiving constructive criticism in a caring
environment is encouraged. Then take time for reflective
evaluation of the feedback before deciding what step
to take next. Nobody understands where you are any
better than you do. So be open minded enough to listen
to suggestions but wise enough to judge what you are
ready for.

6. **Choose a good lesson horse**
Many people don't have the correct horse to help build
their confidence, especially when the person lacks
experience. Just as an apprentice diamond cutter is not
given the highest quality diamonds to learn on, it is not
the best combination for a person who is extremely
unconfident to be learning a new way of horse handling
with a horse that needs a high degree of correct
communication. I'm not suggesting that if a horseman
is having problems with a horse or lacks confidence
they should sell their horse and buy a new one or even
ship it off to a trainer. But I am suggesting progress will
be much faster and confidence will not be destroyed if
they can find supervision and an honest lesson horse
to learn from. A rider with a high level of anxiety and
poor communication skills can ride a confident horse
and get away with it because these horses can fill in
for the person. Even though the person's fear is still
manifest while riding the horse, the rider has at least
completed a safe and successful ride. Each successful

ride multiplies the person's confidence. As experience and confidence expand, a person can become the kind of horseman their tough horse back home needs. A savvy horseman has the talent to cut and buff a challenging horse like a veteran diamond cutter. The top horsemen can transform a horse that is like a diamond in the rough into a real jewel.

7. Choose praise and respect

I have noticed a lot of people beat themselves up about the ability they have with horses or the lack thereof. **But all we can do is the best we can.** None of us have reached perfection. So respect yourself and give yourself a pat on the back for what you can do right now, even if it seems insignificant to others.

As I look back over my horsemanship journey there are some things I did I thought were the best at the time. Later I realized they weren't nearly as good as I thought they were. If I beat myself up about those shortcomings it won't help build my confidence. In fact it will do just the opposite. **All I can do is the best I can right now with the knowledge and skills I have. Then I can allow myself to feel good about it or not.**

If we offer our horses the best we have today then dedicate ourselves to learn more and keep trying, we will have the capacity to offer our horses even better deals. But if we get stuck beating ourselves up for our shortcomings we will miss the opportunity for new knowledge and understanding. If this happens our best won't really be our best.

Choose to praise and respect yourself for being the best you can be. Then realize you can be even better. Just when we think we are the best we can be a horse may come along who teaches us there is still more to learn. This can be a humbling experience. In spite of this you should still praise and respect yourself and your horse in balanced doses. Then offer your horse the best you are at this moment in time and you will be another step closer to winning his heart.

CISCO: The Confidence Builder

Sherry on the trail with Cisco in Wyoming

After an accident on a horse every person needs to rebuild their confidence. No matter how much we try to hide it, fears can creep in after we have been injured. Some people find a way to get over it in almost no time and for others it takes years. There is some truth to the old saying "Get right back on the horse". However, I do not think we should "get right back on" because we think the horse will suppose he has won some kind of battle. I do not believe horses think this way.

The reason we need to wipe the dust off and get back on as soon as physically possible is the sooner we get back on the sooner we will be able to shed the fear before it takes a strong hold on us. The longer the period of time is from a bad riding experience to the next time we ride the harder it will be to get back on. So don't procrastinate.

By getting back on Dolly as soon as I could, I conquered the fear immediately. I knew I didn't have to fear Dolly because I had caused the accident. I understood that unless I had another great lapse of judgment I could reduce the risk of injury in the future by using better savvy. I admitted I had once again reverted to putting my goals before my principles just like I had with Jobe so many years ago. As a result of this incident I now have a lot more HORSE SENSE about me. If I remain true to this HORSE SENSE I won't have to worry about fears creeping back and taking over.

Every person should be so lucky to have a horse like Cisco at least once in their life. I will call him the great confidence booster. He is the horse who escalated my confidence as a horsewoman more than any other horse which has been in my life. Cisco is an undistinguished grade buckskin horse. There is nothing fancy about him on the outside. But on the inside he is much more than mediocre, he is remarkable! We bought him when Dolly was a yearling. He was three years old at the time and very green.

I was teaching school in Wyoming, and Keith was a truck driver. One day he called me at school to tell me he heard about a Buckskin horse for sale on "Tradio" (a radio buy and sell program). I drove over to look at this buckskin horse right after school. I think I knew before I got there I was going to buy him.

A local feed store owner had taken him in trade for a delinquent feed bill. He wasn't having much luck riding him and so the cute buckskin was not much more than a payment of debt. Cisco greeted us at the fence with a friendly and curious look on his face. The owner said, "He really likes people." I tried to ride the untrained buckskin gelding in a round corral. You could say it didn't go very well. I never made it one entire lap around the pen without a buck or an immediate halt and refusal to go forward. Cisco had no stop, no forward, and I couldn't turn him. I asked the owner how much he wanted for his beautiful buckskin colored horse and he said, "$1200". I didn't hesitate or negotiate the price. I wrote out a check for the full amount and said I'd be back on the weekend to pick him up because I didn't have a trailer.

I had always wanted a buck skin colored horse. I know buying a horse simply for color is ridiculous, somehow I couldn't resist. Call it impulse buying or love at first sight, it isn't a very smart reason to write out a check for a horse, but I did it anyway. Fortunately this time I was lucky. Buying Cisco for color and because he liked people turned out to be a good purchase. However, it didn't go smooth from the beginning. We had to work our way into the wonderful partnership we now have.

From the beginning there was just something about this horse's character which intrigued me. Somehow I thought I could trust him with my life, even when he was bucking or running away with me. Even though it sounds impossible, the truth is I have never felt unconfident with him. Everyone who meets him senses there is something exceptional about Cisco. When I ride him I feel so cute because he is so charming. He is a real crowd pleaser during demonstrations, maybe even a bit of a show off. It is very obvious he wants to please, he loves people, and people love him. It doesn't hurt he is a pretty color as well.

I thought it was going to be a piece of cake to win this horse's heart because he had won mine from the moment I laid eyes on him. If this were the only qualification for winning a horse's heart there would be no need for any of us to have to work at being savvy horsemen. The truth is we all have to work hard to become brilliant horsemen who can win a horse's heart. I am no different. Thus began a concentrated schooling period in my horsemanship journey.

Cisco is the first horse I actually rode using a concerted effort to apply better horsemanship principles and techniques. It all started one day while standing in the cold watching kids get on the bus after school. A fellow teacher struck up a conversation with me. He told me I needed to go to this natural horsemanship clinic he was hosting. I didn't even know he rode horses. At first I was a little offended and skeptical even though I tried to hide this truth. What did he mean? I needed to go? How does he know what I need? While I pretended to be listening to him as he talked on and on with excitement about this clinic I stood there thinking: "Why do I need to go to some clinic? I've been riding' since I was two years old. He has never seen me ride. I'm already a good rider." This was true to some extent, my butt sat in a saddle quite well, or so I thought. However my horse handling skills were incomplete even though I was not conscious of it at the time. Later I would even recognize my riding skills needed upgrading.

After he finally convinced me to go watch this clinic I was surprised at how right he was. As I walked away from the clinic I wondered how he had known I needed this opportunity to learn and modify my horsemanship skills. I was both humbled and inspired by the experience. When I talked with him at school on Monday I didn't let on how little I knew about what they were doing at the clinic or the fact that I had learned a lot. However, I couldn't hide my excitement. I was so hungry for more I couldn't wait until the next clinic so I could bring my own horse.

Cisco, Sherry's best buddy

That first clinic revolutionized my thinking. I saw the holes I had in my horsemanship and the reasons for all the frustrations I had for years. There was no turning back now. I jumped in with both feet, wading in over my head. I dedicated myself one hundred percent to this new way. My instructor was making clear the information I had read in books. With her assistance I was able to take this knowledge and apply it in a practical way which worked. Now it was all starting to make sense to me thanks to a friend, a good instructor, and a wonderful horse who would allow it all to happen. I had my dream horse, a Buckskin named Cisco, and a teacher to guide me on this new path. How could I possibly fail?

I'll never forget the first clinic I took Cisco to a month later. I was so enthused until I got there and they told me I was going to have to ride in a skinny little rope halter. What did they mean? Is it really possible to ride a horse without a bit and still have control? What about my tie-down, did I have to leave that off too? Then this crazy person told me she was only giving me one rein to ride with. But it didn't look like a rein to me. It was a twelve foot long, thick, and heavy lead rope. What was I suppose to do with this? I was puzzled and amused at the same time.

All I remember is it was a freezing cold windy March day in Wyoming. By the time we finished all the ground work, which was foreign to me, I was too tired and cold to argue about my bit, tie-down, and riding with only one rein. I put the halter on even though my doubts were great. At least I wasn't afraid of Cisco and we were in an arena. Where was he going to go? I was confident I could ride him as fast as he could run around that arena and he would take care of me. I had recently galloped him as fast as he could run on a dry river bed just for the fun of it and we both survived. So what the heck! What could it hurt? Later I was surprised at how well it went because I didn't have to ride Cisco at high speeds around the arena.

The other thing I remember about that day is the instructor kept yelling at me to sit on my pockets. She instructed me to quit squeezing with my knees and leaning forward. What in the world was she talking about? I sort of ignored her because I didn't think I was doing those things. I even wanted to argue with her. In fact, I think I did once or twice. Later I accepted she was right when I saw myself riding in a video. The interesting thing was when I quit doing those things and started riding more balanced, my knees quit hurting and my horses started responding better.

This instructor convinced me she knew what she was talking about when she asked us to ride straight towards her at a trot and then stop. I did as instructed but my horse didn't stop, and he nearly ran over her. All the while I was thinking, "I didn't think this skinny little rope halter would stop a horse." She told me I needed to stop squeezing with my cheeks and quit riding. I said, "How can you possibly know I am doing that? I have three layers on, long johns, a pair of jeans and coveralls. And on top of that I was facing you. So you couldn't possibly see my butt cheeks." Her reply, "Your horse told me by his response." That was it! She was right! It dawned on me that stopping had nothing to do with the halter or a bit. I acknowledged I knew nothing. I had no focus or *feel* to offer my poor horse because I was so unaware of my own body. Pulling straight back on the rein was telling him one thing while my body was telling him the opposite. It was utter confusion. It's no wonder Cisco didn't stop.

I also had a flash back of a day before this clinic in which Cisco had run away with me. I pulled so hard on both reins trying to stop him that one of my leather reins actually broke. Ooops! Now what do I do? One answer could have been, ride him as fast as he runs. But my muscle memory for thirty years was ingrained in me too deep. Without thinking I did what I always did, pull. As I pulled on the one rein to my utter amazement he started to slow down in a little spiral fashion and he eventually stopped. Hmmmmm! It was my first one rein emergency stop, and it all happened by accident.

I had survived my first clinic. I learned I didn't know as much as I thought I did. Worse yet, I found out I wasn't as good a rider as I thought I was. The only thing I was happy about was Cisco and I had not run over the clinician because she was quick enough to get out of the way. Things were different at home. We didn't have an arena to ride in. We lived on the Wind River Indian Reservation and I rode along the roads, in big fields, or on the huge expanse of BLM land. One day I heard a rumor the people in the area were calling me "The girl who rides horses." When I heard this I thought to myself, "I do ride horses. But what do I really know about it?" If I answered this question with honesty I was a bit embarrassed. How could someone have ridden horses for over thirty years be so unenlightened? I had to admit I needed and wanted to know a whole lot more.

When I was at home by myself I still didn't trust riding in the skinny little rope halter by itself in wide open spaces. With this doubt in my mind I needed a security blanket. So I put my bridle on underneath the rope halter. I rode like that for two months until the next clinic. I put the reins which were attached to the bit over the saddle horn. But I used the lead rope attached to the halter as my rein. After two months I was finally convinced I could use this rope halter and one rein for riding because I had not needed the reins attached to the bit. This persuaded me that control was not about what kind of bit I used or the lack thereof. It was about the *feel* I presented to my horse using my whole body.

This conversion of philosophy gave me a new freedom and independence. Within two years I was riding Cisco naked with confidence just for fun and because I could. This doesn't mean I took my clothes off. Rather Cisco was naked (no saddle or tack on his head). If you had told me this was possible before that day on the play ground watching kids get on the bus when my friend invited me to a clinic, I would have told you, "No way." I remembered my promise to "never do that again" after my wild ride on Jobe many years earlier. So I thought, "What a crazy thing. Why would anyone want to ride a horse bareback and bridleless?" The answer may be, because they can!

Seven years later Cisco was diagnosed with Equine Protozoal Myeloencephalitis (EPM). I was using him at my Horsemanship Camps as a lesson horse. From three year olds to seventy year olds, from girl scouts who had never ridden before to people who were fearful because of serious riding accidents, they were all riding Mr. Dependable. Some just wanted a horse experience, while others needed more confidence, or a better independent seat. Cisco was taking care of all of them. He was teaching a lot of people with different needs and doing it without any complaints.

After one particular camp I went for a relaxing trail ride on Cisco. I like to give him time off from lessons and a training schedule when I can. As I rode him across the hills I could feel he was off. His hindquarters weren't responding or moving correctly. I called a horse chiropractor friend and she thought his alignment was fine. However she was quite sure he had EPM. We were off to the vet the next day. Cisco was hospitalized for about a week. It was very difficult to leave the veterinary clinic. I wanted to sleep there with him until he could come home. This may sound ridiculous, but when a horse has won your heart and in return has permitted you into their heart becoming a part of you there is nothing you won't do for them.

The day I left Cisco at the vet hospital I had a feeling of deep appreciation for all the wonderful moments we have

shared together. I'm sure Cisco doesn't comprehend how
many people's lives he has touched in positive way. This is
what makes him such an extraordinary horse, not just a grade
buckskin pony that was a payment for a debt. Cisco seems to
have recovered from the illness and is doing great now. He
is back in shape for sharing his unique gift of giving riders
confidence because he is tried and true. I will be eternally
grateful to Cisco for being my confidence builder. He is a
piece of good fortune or maybe a stroke of luck in my life.
Either way, he is *not* for sale at any price. If you have ever
had the pleasure to encounter such a horse in your life you
know what I'm talking about.

Competing on Cisco as a 5 year old.

Chapter 7: TIME: Patience vs. Impatience

"I've spent most of my life riding horses; the rest I've just wasted." –unknown

Taking the Time it Takes in the Long Run is Quicker

It is an unfortunate yet true fact that the present environment of the horse industry is rushed in order to meet the demands of an impatient society. It is not uncommon to force horses into quick learning. They are often pushed hard and fast, way too young, causing the slow learners, the fearful or less mature ones to be considered less valuable or even throwaways. Too often when the money is up or the person is frustrated, they simply get rid of the horse that can't keep up under the stress and try another one. Granted, a person can sometimes get away with rushing a horse which has a more tolerant nature. But even these horses must have a solid foundation laid in order to reach their potential.

I don't agree with the use of correction bits or any other mechanical device the sole purpose of which is to speed up the process. Rather I think *feel*, time, and patience are more important elements when developing a willing horse who becomes a lifelong partner. It not only takes the right kind of person to win a horse's heart but a lot of time.

If one wants instant success or instant problem free riding then I suggest they sell their horse sit on the couch with a cup of instant coffee and watch TV. It takes hard work, time, and patience to become a savvy horseman. Anyone who says otherwise isn't being honest.

I have noticed that of all the keys to success with horses, taking the time it takes is the hardest for our generation to accept. Our culture has become accustomed to instant meals, drive throughs, and disposable products. Learning to slow down and take the time it takes will be one of the most difficult changes we make in order to win a horse's heart. But if we do learn this lesson, it will be both valuable and rewarding.

By learning to slow down, not only will the horse learn faster, but both the horse and human will find the whole process more relaxing and enjoyable. Life with a horse will be more peaceful when a slower pace is adopted. When we slow down we will begin to see things we never saw before. As we learn to see through the horse's eyes we are better able to recognize when something is of concern or interest to the horse. With these new eyes we can make more accurate observations, which will give us honest assessments regarding the horse's behaviors and performance. Precise assessments provide us with more effective solutions and guidance.

Knowing When to Quit

I often find myself forgetting about time completely when I'm with a horse. It is unbelievable how fast the hours pass by when one leaves their need to meet a deadline or impress someone behind, replacing it with the prerequisite to do what is best for the horse. Time means nothing to the horseman who is after the heart of a horse. A horseman with this perspective will always put their principles before their own ego and goals. A patient horseman is willing to work right through meals and late into the night until a horse comes around if that is what it takes.

An unselfish horseman is willing to spend months or even years developing the confidence a horse needs in order to perform to their potential with a willing attitude. They won't jeopardize the relationship by doing things they know the horse is not prepared to do. A supportive horseman will do what it takes to prepare the horse in order to set him up for success. Because we are only able to do what the horse is ready for and it is our job to get him ready.

A thoughtful horseman will stop and take the time to figure out why things aren't working, instead of doing the same thing over and over again which isn't working. This reminds me of the image of a horse handler with a death grip on the lead rope right under the horse's chin as if it were a choke collar. Quite often when a person attempts to lead a horse who is being unmanageable for whatever reason in this manner they are dragged or stepped on by the horse. If this happens repetitively, this method of leading a horse may be working for the horse, but it is without a doubt *not* working for the person. It is the horse handler's job to stop and figure out how they can lead a horse with more proficiency. It won't improve if we just keep doing the same thing over and over which isn't working. The benefit of taking the time to figure out why something isn't working is that it will sharpen our ability to know what the horse is going to do before he does it. This will not only improve the relationship, it is the best insurance for staying safe around a horse.

A sharp horseman gives the horse ample wait time. Wait time is a moment or even days to rest and absorb the things he has learned. Rather than moving from one task to the next in rapid succession the horse is given time to digest thoughts by licking and chewing. A clever school teacher uses this principle. If they want all the students in the class to think about an answer to a question, they don't answer the first student who raises his hand before the teacher has even finished asking the question. A teacher who desires to inspire thoughtfulness will give plenty of time for every student to formulate an answer before calling on someone. Learning may only be temporary when things are thrown at us in a hurried sequence, but permanent learning can occur when sufficient time to think is allowed and encouraged.

A watchful horseman knows when to quit and they quit while they are ahead. After a few good attempts it is time to move on before it becomes drill. I've heard people say "just one more time" one too many times. If the horse is bored, exhausted, injured, or in pain then a person quit too late.

Consistent Progression Over Time is Key

A horseman who wants to win a horse's heart will allow for mistakes and baby steps of progression over the course of time. Baby steps take more time to develop than most of us would like to allow. We often expect way too much too soon from a horse. I experienced this myself after a shoulder surgery. My right arm had to be immobile four to six weeks except for a few minimal exercises prescribed by my physical therapist. I am right handed so this presented quite a few new learning opportunities. Even though I was very familiar with the tasks I wanted my left hand to do, it just wouldn't cooperate. It was as if my hand wanted to obey my brain signals but it couldn't figure out the pattern. Even after a hundred tries it still didn't feel natural doing things with my left hand. My will to use my left hand was there, but the coordination was missing.

If we can't do something new well the first time why do
we think a horse can? Don't   expect the horse to do things
perfectly right away. Instead give the horse plenty of time
to make baby steps. With sufficient time and good practice
the brain will communicate to the body with more clarity.
The body will learn to respond appropriately to the clear
brain signals. As this happens coordination will improve and
the necessary muscles will develop so the tasks can become
effortless. I know this works because before the six weeks
had passed I drew a nice-looking picture of a mustang with
my left hand. A task I definitely thought was impossible,
because before this time I could hardly hold a pencil with
my left hand. This leads me to believe that no matter what
bad habits or baggage your horse has, there is hope. We
can develop new positive patterns of behavior and further
accomplishments with our horse if we are willing to allow
for baby steps over time.

When we allow for baby steps it means we praise or reward
the smallest effort. Remember the praise or rewards we offer
the horse have to have explicit value to horse. A horse is not
looking for the same kind of praise a human may desire.

Most humans are motivated by such things as affection (I love
you), faith (I believe), verbal praise (Atta Boy), recognition
(titles and awards), material objects (money, toys, food,
etc.), enjoyment (vacations, fun, etc.) power, greed, or sex.
There are many other reasons humans are motivated to do
anything, but for most animals, especially the horse, it isn't
that complicated. Most of the things that motivate a horse
are related to survival because they are a prey animal. Their
main motivators are safety first (Are you going to kill or eat
me?) A close second is comfort (When the wind is blowing
sleet and rain and I can't find adequate protection I put my
butt to the wind). Food can be pretty high on the list (When

and what can I eat?) Reproduction is cyclical (Procreation for survival is a natural instinct I can't help but go along with.) Curiosity is also meaningful (I love to explore and investigate my surroundings so I know when to escape or when to fool around.) And finally, play (If I feel safe and comfortable then curiosity allows me freedom to amuse myself. There are a variety of ways I engage in play, from running, bucking, tearing things up, opening things with my mouth, to sparring with my buddy.) Many horsemen forget that a horse can find a lot of value in the human doing nothing. One of the best rewards for a horse when he has done something terrific is, leave him alone. LET HIM BE! DO NOTHING!

In the long run, slow and right is actually faster because you don't have to keep fixing the same problem over and over again. By slowing down we will get permanent results. Cures take time, effort, patience, and knowledge. Impatient people who want a quick fix for every problem will get temporary results at best and at worst they may cause permanent damage to the horse. It is like losing weight. Diet pills may give you a quick weight loss, but pills alone won't permanently cure a weight problem. One has to change their lifestyle to keep the weight off. The diet you stick with is the one which works. Remember slow, gradual, and consistent progression will help build good habits, confidence, and understanding. Praise or rewards for the slightest try, which are suitable to a horse, motivate him to accept our leadership. Permanent positive behavior changes and better overall performance are the result of systematically using these logical guidelines.

Quick Fixes Don't Produce Permanent Changes

I am reminded of a personal experience which demonstrates why overexposure and rushing rarely result in a better performance. I grew up in central Nebraska in a very rural community. The first time I drove in a town with a stop light I was twenty-six years old. My first experience of city driving was very traumatic because I was forced into it without any preparation or realistic expectations. It was much harder than I thought it would be and to this day it still isn't easy for me. My husband at the time and I flew to Dallas for a conference. He had let his driver's license expire and we needed to rent a car. Since he didn't have a license, I was forced to drive. Oh boy, this caused a major attack of nerves and stress for me. As I drove my knuckles were white and I had severe heart palpitations. My body was tense and shaking all over. When we stopped the car I had what I call sewing machine legs. It was an excessive nerve-racking experience for me. To this day I still experience degrees of anxiety when driving in a big city.

I would have a lot more confidence in my ability to drive in a city if I had prepared myself for the challenge through gradual steps, rather than throwing myself on a freeway with numerous lanes without any skills. If I had prepared myself by driving shorter periods in a smaller city in order to build my confidence, I am sure my first experience would not have been so terrifying. I still get sewing machine legs, shake like a leaf and get heart palpitations every time I think about driving through an unfamiliar city.

The point is we need to understand a horse's insecurities and give him the time he needs to build his confidence so he can do what we ask with success. We can build his confidence by gradually putting him into situations he perceives as unsafe instead of expecting him to handle every situation immediately without incident. I don't think we realize how hard it can be for a horse to do some of the things we expect him to do. Some people may think asking a person to drive through a city is not a big deal. But to people like

me it is more than a big deal. In fact it can be perceived as
life threatening not just dangerous. When a horse is in self-
preservation mode, rushing them by using quick fixes will
only scare the horse more. It won't convince him we know
what we are doing. Being hasty can cause further confusion,
more resistance, and injuries are more common if we don't
take the time it takes.

Here are a couple of examples of quick fixes we should *not*
consider if we want to win our horse's heart. I have also
included alternative solutions which can take more time but,
from the horse's point of view, work better.

Rearing and Clubs

Some people think the answer to a rearing horse is to club
him between the ears. As long as the person holds the club
the horse may not rear because he is afraid of the pain to
follow. We must not forget that this is punishment because
it happens after the fact. It is too late to have a positive effect
on the horse and it causes even more alarm in the horse.
An approach which is more fitting to the horse occurs right
before or at the beginning of the action in order to change the
horse's behavior pattern. This builds his confidence.

Why Does a Horse Rear?

As we seek to be safe with horses, it is just as important
to know why the horse rears as knowing what to do about
it. If we know why a horse rears, then the best solution is
to do something to prevent it in the first place. Being able
to recognize behaviors which indicate it may happen is the
only way we can prevent such extreme behavior. A horse
expresses his displeasure or fear through body language.
Rearing just happens to be one of many, like swishing tail,
ears back, crabby look, tight mouth, not wanting to come to

you, running away, throwing head in the air, hollowing the back, bucking, fighting against pressure, being herd bound, muscle tension, not being able to look at you, shutting down, a vacant or disinterested look, etc. This is all just feedback for us. No matter what the horse does we must accept the fact if we are with him his behavior, either positive or negative, does have something to do with us. It is our responsibility to make things better for the horse.

The type of brutal and unnecessary punishment described above does not address or solve the reason behind the rearing problem. The typical reasons a horse rears are he is confused, afraid, or feeling too confined. A horse will rear when they don't want to go forward for whatever reason and the person blocks all other avenues of movement. Consider the opposite when the horse wants to go forward and the rider forces the horse backwards with too much pressure. In either case rearing becomes an attempt to move away from or get rid of too much pressure on either reins or a lead rope. Whatever the reasons behind rearing, a horse is in full panic mode when he resorts to this action.

Rearing is often connected to pulling away from what the horse does *not* understand. It is a normal reaction to his claustrophobic tendencies or when too much force is being used. Rearing can be taught as a result of confusion. We need to ask ourselves: "What am I doing to contribute to the horse's misunderstanding? How can I give the horse some slack? How can I change my presentation to clear up these misunderstandings?"

When the horse is frightened the rider often becomes afraid as well. A rider's first response to their own fear is very often to block the horse from moving forward by pulling back on both reins at the same time. This is a very bad idea because the

brace in the human's body pulling on both reins presents an
unsolvable bind for the horse whose body is already braced in
self-preservation. The horse becomes stiff through his jaws,
neck, back, and hindquarters. Therefore it is not possible for
him yield to the pressure in a proper way. With all of this
rigidity throughout the horse's body it will be very difficult
to influence his hind quarters, which is what we need to be
able to do to resolve the problem. Plus, by pulling back on
two reins we have transferred all his weight to the hind legs.
This sets the horse up in the perfect balanced position to rear.
What the horse really needs is to calm down and establish a
new point of balance. This new point of balance can be found
on the diagonal legs instead of his two hind legs. We can help
the horse achieve this new point of balance by allowing the
feet to move forward.

Finding the Open Door, Relief of Pressure

When a rider never provides the proper release in the reins,
up is the only way the horse has to relieve the pressure.
Relief of pressure is what every horse lives for. If we do not
provide this release each and every time we ask the horse to
do anything, then the horse will seek it himself. This is the
very basics of training. Every horseman seeking *feel* should
burn this into their mind until it is instinctual for them to
operate in this way. To put it in very simple terms, we allow
the pressure to make it easier for the horse to find the one
open door which provides release. However, we had better
make sure this is the door we want him to go through. It is
important to show the horse there's always a way out and that
he's not trapped. I think the release is more important than
the pressure. A better way of thinking about it might be to
focus on moving the horse *into* softness rather than moving
him *away* from pressure.

This concept of pressure/release works whether we are conscious of the process or not. The horse is always operating from this premise whether we are or not. Even if they don't realize it, some people teach their horses to rear because of this process. When the rider doesn't provide the proper release, the horse will look for relief somewhere else. If up is where the horse finds a release then that is what he will do. When the horse discovers the only open door is up, the person should not be puzzled about why it is not what they wanted. To a perceptive horseman it is obvious the horse did what he needed to do to find the release.

The worst part of a quick fix (clubbing a horse between the ears) is that a person can cause serious and permanent injury or even death to the horse. Even if physical injury isn't apparent it will cause emotional instability in the horse. More than likely it will take a long time to gain the horse's trust back and his confidence may never be the same again. This could be an example of one of those pivotal moments I spoke of earlier.

The slow but permanent solution to this problem is proper preparation. This means taking the time it takes to teach the horse to respond quickly and softly to one rein by giving his head to the side then disengaging his hindquarters. (This means the inside hind leg steps under the body, crossing the other hind leg). Then we need to establish forward movement because a horse cannot rear with forward movement and the hindquarters stepping out. It is also important to expose the horse to as many things as you can during his foundation training. This is done by educating the horse to relax and trust the handler's guidance. I use lots of ground games and puzzles for the horse to solve which when done correctly will teach the horse to trust humans and control his fears. Again this is not a how-to book about particular training exercises. In the

back of this book there is a list of recommended programs
which can teach you specific methods and techniques to help
your horse be smarter and braver.

The Best Solution is Prevention and Prior Preparation

In some cases when we are in too deep the only solution is
to abort, regroup, and start over before somebody gets hurt.
We all know that whenever we are out of control of a horse
we are in danger! We shouldn't be on a horse if we don't
have the lead or if we are in a defensive position trying
to hold back on the reins in order to just stay on as things
continue to get worse. We must be ready to get off at any
time when things degenerate beyond our capabilities. This
is not something most people think of until it's too late. I
don't believe we should try to stay on a horse no matter
what. Nor should we tolerate unsafe or silly behaviors from
a horse. When a horse is out of control it is imperative that
we are not trying to teach him something or accomplish a
complex task. Instead we need to focus on interrupting the
behavioral pattern so we can regain control of the horse's
mind. If that means getting off so we can get the job done
then there is no dishonor in that.

Being brave does not mean setting your jaw to do something
anyway even if you know it is not a good idea. I've seen
a lot of people get hurt that way because they just didn't
have the experience required to handle the situation. Even
though they knew this they pressed on. We may never
understand all the reasons why a person doesn't stop when
they should have. The fact still remains, a horseman who
ignores all the signs and quits too late will have to live
with the consequences. We also have to understand some
horsemen may be riding a horse which looks to be out of

control to us. It depends on the rider's leadership ability, experience, mental, emotional, and physical fitness level as to how much they can handle before they feel they are in danger. Knowing your own abilities is part of being a confident leader. I realize even the experienced confident leader can misjudge a situation and get hurt, so we must not beat ourselves up when we make such a mistake.

Riding is much more than trying to manage chaos. We don't need to just manage or tolerate rearing. We can do more than just survive rearing, we can learn to prevent and *fix* it. It is necessary to do more than treat the symptoms of rearing. We have to dig deep to discover the cause so we can cure the problem. The more we know and practice preventative medicine, the safer we will be. We have to stop being a reactive rider and start being a proactive rider.

The best solution is prevention. If we are aware of potential problems sometimes we can just eliminate the pressure which is causing the problem. This is better than waiting until the horse is out of control. It is better to catch the horse before he rears, and do something about it right then. This takes a very diligent rider who is always paying attention to his horse. In order to do this we have to become an expert in feeling the body motion a horse will take before he rears.

Before a horse rears he will shorten the length of his hind step so that he can transfer his point of balance to his hind legs. There will be a feeling of reluctance to go which will cause him to stiffen his body and raise his head. It is like his hind feet are stuck in mud, and his front end will start to feel light. As soon as you feel this, immediately, without hesitation bend his head with one rein and disengage his hindquarters, then move him on out forward. If we will learn to anticipate this dangerous problem by staying aware at all times of the signs leading up to it, and prepare the horse beforehand we can eliminate rearing without severe punishment.

Trailers, Ropes, Blindfolds, and Bribery

I believe more horses lose their dignity and trust in humans with quick-fix trailer loading tactics than any other activity. Not to mention how many are injured physically and mentally. A very small sampling of these tactics include use of all kinds of ropes tied in various ways in order to force a horse in the trailer, the use of an actual winch, blindfolding a horse, and bribery with treats.

I recently heard of a horse that was blindfolded and forced into a trailer. This poor horse ended up crawling into the trailer on his front knees. Even though this person did get his horse into the trailer in a short amount of time, there is no way this horse will get into a trailer on his own accord the next time this person attempts to load him. Because the person didn't really teach the horse anything about trailer loading except maybe to distrust humans even more. This technique should only be used as a last resort in case of an extreme emergency situation when there is no other choice. In the world's worst situation a blindfolded horse will follow the leader because he really has no other option. I have never used this technique and I plan not to. Nor would I ever recommend. A wise horseman will be prepared for anything instead of relying on techniques which don't require skill and effective communication. A horseman who wants to win his horse's heart understands how important it is to teach his horse to be confident with trailer loading *before* an emergency situation arises. When this viewpoint is implemented it is not necessary to resort to these kinds of tactics.

The main reason horse handlers have so many problems with trailer loading is they have not taken the time to prepare their horse. Because they have not prepared their horse in advance when they have to go somewhere they resort to the quick fix. The next time they have to load the horse it is even more problematic. It is difficult because they didn't address the real problems, which are the horse's claustrophobic tendencies and the lack of trust, respect, and communication between the horse and the human. In fact the quick fix has caused even less trust, respect and communication between the horse and the human. So now, we have to work even harder to get it back.

There are two main ingredients a horse needs in order to convince him to get into a trailer on his own accord. First the horse needs to have enough respect for the handler to move his body forward with little or no hesitation when given a proper cue which the horse can understand. Second the horse needs confidence to face a very claustrophobic situation. A horse will have more confidence if he trusts the handler as a competent leader who will not force or trick him into the trailer using fear or intimidation tactics. Without respect and trust which lead to obedience and confidence we end up with nothing more than frustration or worse yet, accidents which lead to injuries for both the horse and the human.

A Forward Cue, Simulations, and Confidence Lead to Successful Trailer Loading

The first thing we must establish before ever approaching the trailer is a good forward cue. I will call this cue "the send". This is not about leading the horse by the head but asking the horse to move forward from the shoulders toward a designated place with intention and energy. There are two main keys to easy trailer loading: Well-mannered, lively, forward motion from the horse upon request and never requesting more forward motion when the horse is already trying.

Part of the preparation before asking a horse into a trailer is to simulate the action of trailer loading in many creative ways. Here are some ideas: Over a wooden bridge forward and backwards, jumping a log or barrel, put the horse's front feet up on a pedestal or tarp, cross a tarp, ditch, or water, go through a small gate, a door, or between trees that are close together with low hanging branches. The better a horse will send over all of these things the more willingly, confidently and respectfully the horse will respond when asked to load in a trailer. Make a game of it and have some fun with purpose.

It is essential to have the proper attitude with plenty of time when loading a horse in a trailer. If we become angry, frustrated, anxious, or nervous the horse will catch our spirit. Then he will reflect those same emotions in his own behavior. When we are in a big hurry the horse may become even more reluctant. Remember horses hate to be rushed into anything. We need to be very matter-of-fact acting, as if we are going nowhere important. Ask the horse to get into the trailer as if nothing unusual is going on just like he has done it well a thousand times before. Above all we must remember to relax and take our time. We can't rush a horse into a trailer hoping he will be in before he knows what has happened to him. Give the horse some credit. He is smarter and more perceptive than that.

With prior and proper preparation, trailer loading doesn't have to be a traumatic or difficult experience for either the horse or the handler. If we have done our homework we will be armed with a good forward cue, confidence, and the proper attitude. With plenty of time we will be able to convince the horse to load in the trailer on their own accord. A simple point of a finger will eventually be all it takes.

What's the Hurry?

Remember it's not about the trailer but about the relationship and good communication. Are you able to communicate with your horse in a manner he understands? Are you a task master, never giving your horse a moment's peace to absorb what has just happened? Do you expect overnight success? Are you in a big hurry all the time? Or can you take the attitude that I don't care if this takes two minutes, two hours, two days or two years. I will do what it takes to build my horse's confidence, trust and respect and therefore win his heart with my patience.

Remember, time is a precious thing we will never get back, so when you are with your horse make the most of every moment. Quit worrying about where you need to rush off to next, because your horse will feel the competition going on within you causing a disjointed focus. Thinking about what you need to do after your horse time is over is cheating yourself and your horse of a rich and full experience.

Think about it, "What's your hurry?" You aren't going to get more accomplished in a day by squashing too many things into the precious few hours you are blessed to have with your horse, nor will it improve or hasten his training. There is no need for a hurry up and get'r done now attitude in the training arena. It will only stress out most horses. In fact, unhurried, simple, and gentle requests create clear communication which will result in more positive responses from a horse. Quit zooming around like a hummingbird on crack, take a deep breath and relax. Let go of any anxiety about what you think you need to accomplish. Make a concerted effort to leave the stress of life behind when you approach the barn. Many people say spending time with their horse is what keeps them happy or sane. So make it a habit to give the same peace to your horse by slowing down and consciously asking your horse for things in a calmer manner. The effect on your horse will be profound.

One last helpful suggestion about time: When you go to the barn to be with your horse, try to schedule two hours for every task you think will take one hour. Like most projects it seems everything takes twice as long and costs twice as much as you expect. For me, two hours is about the minimum for a visit with a horse no matter what I am planning to do.

On the same theme, I never take my cell phone or any other thing with me to the barn or arena which will cause me to want to multi-task. When I schedule a time in my busy life for our horses, it is our time. If at all possible I do not accept anything other than a true emergency as an interruption. This may sound like I am too serious or even rude, but my time is limited. The time I can spend with our horses is precious, so I intend to make the most of every moment. There is nothing wrong with spontaneity. If all I can do is squeeze in a few minutes a day in with our horses, I will take advantage of those opportunities as well. However, if a horse lover really wants to become great with horses it takes a dedication where more than spontaneity is required. Consistent and quality time in an unhurried manner will pay the best dividends and you will surely win a horse's heart.

SUNSHINE Prayers of Patience

"Our patience will achieve more than our force."
                    -- Edmund Burke

Sunshine trusting Sherry
(Photographer Julie Williams)

Even though Sunshine, a bay tobiano, has been a challenge, she has taught me more about myself than any other horse. Some might say she had a bad attitude from the day she hit the ground. She is the kind of horse which could ruin a horse lovers dream or take you way beyond them. Sunshine was given to us. It was her last chance for a good life.

When Sunshine came to live with us she was five years old and quite aggressive. Her painted black, white and brown spots made her appearance quite striking. However, her crabby personality didn't seem to match her physical beauty.

She had been nicknamed Taz, short for the Tasmanian devil because of her undesirable attitudes and behaviors.

Sunshine was not fond of human predators in any shape, gender, or size. She had chased people out of a corral, as she believed she was trying to save her own life. I can imagine her teeth bared running head on toward someone. Then realizing she was not going to stop, I can see a person scrambling up and over the fence in a frantic attempt to escape. Maybe they even lost a hat, a boot, or tore clothing as they reach the top and plunged to safety on the other side of the fence.

Out of breath with heart pounding, the victim turns to see a very misunderstood mare who isn't winning any popularity contests. She is snorting and blowing through her red-hot flared nostrils. Her head and tail are held high. Sunshine's bulging eyes are filled with more fear than hatred. The adrenaline is flowing through her blood at the same high speed it is flowing through the person panting in disgust on the other side of the fence. Both are equally afraid but have dealt with their fear in very different ways.

Sunshine didn't know how to control herself because her natural instinct for survival had taken complete control of her mind and emotions. She was at the point where she would do anything to ensure her own safety and comfort, including hurt someone if they got in the way. She was so out of control she could have even hurt or killed herself in a panic. When she was in this state her brain and all thinking faculties were over-ridden by her extreme fear. My goal was to show her my affection and care in order to win her trust, thus eliminating her need to deal with her fears in an aggressive manner. It would be many months before she was ready to trust me.

It was not safe to pet Sunshine without a halter on, even from the other side of the fence. She would lay her ears back, try to bite, then turn her hindquarters towards me and kick. It was intimidating. She knew how to get her point across. Some people saw her as a naughty or mean horse. But in reality, Sunshine was in her own little world of pain and fear. She couldn't be a partner to anyone until she learned to control her emotions and fear. Sunshine was already very sensitive but confidence is what she needed more than anything else.

I had heard people say, "Someday she is going to kill someone". But all I saw was a frightened horse who was trying to survive by defending herself. Sunshine was difficult to catch without grain, because this was a habit developed at her previous home. I choose to allow my horses to catch me instead of tricking, bribing, or trapping them. However, in order to help Sunshine feel some sense of familiarity, I continued to use the bribe of grain to catch her for a couple of weeks. Once she was caught her behavior did improve. At least she wasn't so aggressive, although she was still elusive, spooky, and disrespectful.

One of the main problems with Sunshine was she was head shy to the point of being dangerous. She would toss and shake her head with violence then back away at a high speed whenever I tried to touch her head near the poll or ears. Her right ear was the most sensitive and it was a no man's land. Even a slight brush of it would send her rearing and striking. This made her difficult to halter, and normal bridling was out of the question.

I was also informed Sunshine had developed the dangerous habit of rearing while being ridden, especially when she was frightened, which seemed to be most of the time. I caught her more than once practicing this skill while by her self in a corral or stall. She was scared of her own shadow. Nevertheless, I dreamed of having a safe and fun relationship with this strong willed yet very fragile mare.

I began playing with her in the round pen at liberty. There were times I was glad I had my horseman stick because she charged me a few times. I didn't back down. But I didn't punish her either because I knew it would only add fuel to her fire. Plus I wanted her trust as much as her respect. I was determined to win her heart, not break her spirit.

Little by little things improved. One thing which didn't improve was the head-shy issue. Poor Sunshine would grind her teeth, contort her facial expressions, duck, and flip her head, or twist it side to side in an odd manner when she was uncomfortable with anything around her head. She didn't leave out her defensive behavior of rearing and striking when I tried to get her accustomed to various objects around her head like halters, ropes, headstalls, brushes, etc.

Since most horse dreams involve riding, I thought I had to ride Sunshine right away. Of course our first ride didn't go as well as I had planned. She was very cranky and full of resistance. I rode her in a round pen using a rope halter. She kept jerking her head like a nose fly was biting her even though the reins were loose and there was not a nose fly within a hundred miles. I later discovered she was not only over sensitive to touch on top of her head but below her chin as well.

When I asked her to flex laterally it felt like she was a cannon ready to explode. The confinement was too much for her because she was an extreme claustrophobic. She was scared out of her wits and maybe I should have been also. At least she didn't rear, so I believed we were making progress even though her face and neck were contorted in a tense and odd fashion.

I rode her several more times. I knew inside I was stealing rides and that I was sitting on a walking time bomb. I should have been developing a better relationship and line of communication with her on the ground before expecting her to trust and respect me on her back. As luck would have it, an unforeseen intervention helped keep me safe. The circumstance also granted us the time we needed to develop our relationship before I continued riding her.

One day I was grooming Sunshine in preparation for a ride. Every time I stroked her softly with the brush on her shoulder she tried to bite me. Her head was as high as she could hold it, her eyes were wild and she was in hyper-defensive self-preservation mode. She would not even accept the gentle touch of my hand. Somewhat puzzled by her behavior, instead of fighting her, I put her away for the day. I thought we had been making a little progress with trust between us, apparently I was wrong.

The next day Sunshine was not better. This time I noticed what appeared to be blisters on her shoulders. Then I also saw similar blisters on her back legs and neck. It seemed poor Sunshine was sunburned wherever she had white hair. No wonder she wouldn't let me touch her, she was in terrible pain. Her medical condition also began to show up in other ways. She was stiff while trying to move and her stools became dry and hard which caused her to strain.

We lived in Wyoming at the time and there was not an abundance of grass hay so we fed straight alfalfa. After some research we discovered Sunshine was suffering from an extreme case of photosensitivity disease. Her liver was not functioning properly with the amount of high-protein-rich feed she was ingesting. Her body was overflowing with toxins. The only cure was to change her feed and no exposure to the sun until the burns healed and her hair grew back. I was advised to put Sunshine down but I couldn't do it.

Sunshine with confidence to jump.
(Photographer Julie Williams)

For the next nine months Sunshine lived in the barn during the day out of the sun, only going outside after dark. As the days continued she lost all of her beautiful white hair from the peeling sunburned skin. It fell off in chunks. She didn't seem to mind as I picked off the dead skin and hair. As she ate her special hay, to her delight I rubbed vitamin E oil and aloe vera on her tender new skin to sooth it. Before this time Sunshine was very aggressive when she was eating. Humans were not tolerated within thirty feet of her food without some kind of admonition to stay away. I felt she may have understood I was trying to help her. Maybe she was beginning to trust me, laying aside some of her fears and defensive behaviors. At any rate we were taking some significant steps forward toward developing a partnership.

I couldn't ride Sunshine until her hair grew back. So during this time we played ground games on line and at liberty in the round pen in the dark. We also spent plenty of non-demanding time together, just hanging out enjoying each other's company. We went for walks down the road together and sometimes I walked alongside her in the pasture as she grazed. Everything we did was very low key, slow, and repetitive, mixed with lots and lots of reward. The most rewarding thing for Sunshine was when I stood beside her and left her alone, giving her time to relax and soak it all up. We spent a lot of quality time together without any high expectations.

I was still anxious to ride Sunshine but I'm glad I was forced to stay off her back until her skin was healed. It gave us both the time we needed to learn about each other. Our hearts and minds began to make an exclusive connection. A lot of emotional and mental healing went on during this very important time, which set us up for success for the day when I would climb on her back again.

When it was time to ride her again I pretended as if she was an un-started colt even though she was seven years old and had previous riding experience. I started at the beginning in order to rebuild a solid foundation of trust, respect, and basic skills. This created an environment of safety and comfort for both of us. With this foundation I hoped to reveal the true horse within which I knew was just waiting to get out. As I looked into her soft brown eyes I knew I wouldn't be complete until I had developed a healthy partnership with this unique horse. As we have gained confidence in one another it has satisfied an inner longing of unconditional love for both of us.

I dreamed of riding Sunshine with grace over hills and valleys, through rivers and forests. I also envisioned jumping logs and fences with balance, coordination and a perfect sense of timing with her. I hoped we would learn to move together with perfect harmony because we could anticipate each others actions. I sought to understand Sunshine so that she could respond with eagerness to my guidance. I anticipated a time when my desires would become hers and vice versa. I sensed that if we ever became one, Sunshine would carry me to new heights of freedom. But at this stage in our relationship we still had a lot of mountains to climb. However, I was sure there was no mountain too high for us to conquer.

As of the writing of this book I do ride Sunshine over hills and valleys with our own sense of harmony and freedom. It has taken a lot longer to get where we are than I expected it to. It may take even longer to reach all the lofty goals I want to achieve with Sunshine. I'm not worried about this because time is one thing we are blessed with. I am going to use every minute I have with Sunshine to enhance what we already have. We haven't conquered rivers, forests and mountains yet, but we have a good start in understanding each other. No matter whether we reach these aspirations or not I am content that we will be life-long partners enjoying the journey together. As in all relationships I am positive we will still have our highs and lows. We probably won't be winning any gold medals soon, but that doesn't seem to make any difference in our relationship. What does carry some weight is we are both changed for the better for having traveled this journey together.

I had a special time with Sunshine recently which indicated to me I may have won her heart. We had our first snowstorm of the season at the end of Oct. Our horses are only stalled during bad weather. So we put them in for the night. The next morning in my usual fashion I opened the stall doors allowing the horses to leave as they pleased. Everyone left the barn except Sunshine. I encouraged her out the door to join her friends a couple of times, but she kept coming back. Well, maybe she only wanted the comfort of the barn and a little more hay. However, it had warmed up considerably outside so it wasn't necessary for her comfort. Plus her belly must have been full after two hours of eating even though horses seem to be bottomless pits when it comes to food. The thing that makes me believe it was more than comfort and food was she followed me to each stall. Then she just stood there watching me as I scooped manure. She had to have been getting thirsty since we don't have water in the barn. We hand water each horse as needed because the hours they spend in the barn are minimal. All the other horses went straight to the tank for a drink when turned out. I would like to believe she enjoyed just hanging out with me in the barn. I in turn was honored by her presence and the trust she has finally placed in me.

My parents taught me when I was a little girl that we must be able to give before we can receive. We will receive joy, pleasure, and satisfaction if we learn how to win a horse's heart by giving. These very emotions were overflowing to me that morning as I picked manure in the presence of an unexpected friend who I will cherish forever. The silent peace in the barn which existed between us was a gift I am thrilled to have experienced, especially since there were times I doubted whether it would ever happen. I don't believe it happened because of me and who I am, but because of Sunshine and who she is.

I see the world from a different perspective when mounted on Sunshine. While seated on her back time stands still. All of my troubles seem minor in comparison to what she must encounter in her mind and emotions when she gets troubled. No matter how treacherous and challenging the trail has been with Sunshine she has taught me the invaluable lessons of selflessness, empathy, and patience every step of the way. These qualities of giving are the most important qualities one must posses in abundance in order to win a horse's heart. The brutal honest feedback provided by Sunshine has been my best guide to the truth or falsehood about whether I possessed these qualities. Through her I have learned that good horsemanship is so much more than technique or mechanics. It is something that comes from within.

I think it is very important to recognize the potential in every horse and then give them the opportunity to reveal it from within. There comes a moment of recognition, when we know things are right and true. I know when things are right for Sunshine because she looks confident, elegant, and secure. When this happens she chooses to be deep in concentration, she experiments with her body movements and is happy in the work I am asking her to perform. Everyone can see it when things are right; it doesn't take a trained eye. On the other hand it can be hard to see what is missing when things are not right. Trying to find what was missing for Sunshine, figuring out how to draw out her latent talents, and teach her required skills for riding have been the greatest challenges I have had in developing a relationship with her.

Through the years with Sunshine I discovered that deep within this troubled horse is an imprisoned wealth of magnificent character qualities. The graceful talent buried beneath her rough and tough physical exterior did not need to be developed but instead liberated. Before the true horse could shine through in her I had to dig deep down within myself. When I did, I found many things in my own character which needed rooting out or at least modified in order to understand how to help Sunshine relieve her tension and heal her scars. Through the process we both have been liberated to be who we are, expressing our talents with unreserved passion. Well, maybe me more than Sunshine, but I hope to continue to lead the way for her.

Riding Sunshine in a halter at her first Women's Camp.

With continuous observations, constant experimentation, and the gentle techniques I have learned with natural horsemanship, I have begun to open all sorts of ways for Sunshine's imprisoned splendor to escape into favorable expression. At first positive expression from her was limited, timid, and confined because of the newness of the experience. Now she is beginning to be more spontaneous, exuberant, and abundant with cheerful expressions. The defensive horse who was really terrified of everything is starting to share more of her real self with me. It is this unrestricted sharing of her real self which has enabled me to accomplish more with her than some thought possible. It is not my perfect technique or horsemanship talent which has brought about this change in her, but my willingness to allow her to be the horse she is. As I aimed to bring out her best qualities she has brought out mine. Our hearts will be bound together forever.

MEANDERING WITH SUNSHINE IN THE SHADE

The late July sun was beaming sultry,
A gentle breeze came from the southeast,
Which made it comfortable in the shade,
Where I took the lovely painted beast.

"Sunshine" as the mare was named,
Came to me full of insecurities & fears,
As we have developed our relationship,
It has been full of both joy and tears.

As we left the corral through the front gate,
The first bite of grass was full of pain,
When a yellow jacket stung her on the nose,
I didn't blame her for shaking her mane.

We meandered through the front yard,
Investigating things which gave her a scare,
Each time moving closer & staying longer,
Remembering our game must always be fair.

Every threshold of real or perceived danger,
Together we were able to defeat,
It helped build her confidence & curiosity,
And now we felt a bit more complete.

The Frisbee the dog loves to fetch,
She observed & approached with caution,
Until finally she stomped it assertively,
Securing her self-preservation.

In the living-room picture window,
She saw another beautiful horse,
Whom she greeted warmheartedly,
Then neighed when she left, of course.

Now that Sunshine is learning to be brave,
Soon she will be able to outshine the rest,
Because lying dormant inside her,
Is a partner that wants to be the very best!

Sherry Jarvis 7-20-05

FINAL THOUGHTS

"When pride rideth in the saddle, destruction rideth on the crupper."(Author unknown)

The Journey Continues

Continuing any journey will be both laboring and joyful. Everything in life seems to follow some kind of cycle. I have noticed there seems to be a pattern or cycle of learning as we continue these journeys. The first two steps in the pattern, Excitement and Realization Coupled With Doubt, are considered beginnings. There are people who love the thrill of beginnings and others are not very fond of them. Those who dislike beginnings may do so because they would rather get lost somewhere in the middle where things don't change much. Some people may get so hooked on beginnings they never finish anything.

The middle stage includes Acceptance and Searching For Advice, and Trust And Hard Work. Many people want to give up at this point because they prefer the excitement of the beginning or the satisfied feeling of the ending. It can be easy to have trouble in the middle when the newness wears off and the day-to-day grind becomes reality. However, some people love the middle because they can feel the process. They love the security of the sameness and day-to-day structure the middle can offer. Other people love the middle because they are procrastinators who never want to finish anything.

Whether you enjoy the middle or not, the fact is, the middle usually takes the longest and involves a lot of perseverance, consistency, repetition, practice, and patience.

There are those who can't wait to get to the finish line. In the final phase a Breakthrough gives us Joy. A feeling of completion or a sense of accomplishment for a job well done can be very rewarding. The ending of one project nearly always presents a new avenue of travel. When we take on the challenge of a new direction the cycle begins all over again. By setting out on another new learning journey our growth never stops.

If I had to put myself into a category I might say I am a "beginning" person. To me it is more about the relationships developed along the way than it is about the final destination. However, I have learned to appreciate all chapters of the journey. There is a certain gratification throughout the whole process when we are willing to change gears as we pass through each turning point. It makes the ride a lot smoother. If we take care of our horsemanship then it will take care of us.

The following is a further explanation of the seven steps we experience as we continue the journey:

1. EXCITEMENT!
   Most journeys begin with a lot of excitement as we anticipate the opportunities the trip may present. It can be very exciting when we buy a new horse, get a new job, expect a first child, or set out on a voyage to someplace we have never been before. Many people enjoy the excitement of beginnings when everything is new and untarnished. They dream of the many possibilities. Others don't enjoy beginnings because of the fear of the

unknown. They may be too busy looking at the "what ifs". The beginning of any venture is often filled with both fears and joyfulness. Either way you look at it there is a lot to prepare for during this first stage of the journey. The expectations are both exciting and stressful as one makes preparations for a new journey.

2. REALIZATION COUPLED WITH DOUBT

A person may start out thinking how exciting this new event will be, but this thinking is often followed with feelings of doubt, like: *"What did I get myself into? Can I do this?"* or *"Why am I here?"*

This reality check, followed by doubt, often goes something like this: I have my first horse or a new horse. It's reality. But now what? Doubts grow even bigger if things don't go as you dreamed, or seem harder than you ever imagined them to be. You go to a clinic and thoughts like these start going through your head. *I've made a mistake. This is too advanced or too easy for me. Maybe I don't need this stuff. I do need this stuff but I'm not ready for all of this yet.*

3. ACCEPTANCE AND SEARCHING FOR ADVICE

The next stage is when the person begins to settle into the fact that this journey is a reality. Even though they have some doubts about it and their abilities they realize they may as well make the best of the situation. First you accept the fact you don't know all there is to know about owning a horse, riding, having a baby, or the skills needed for a new job, etc. Since you don't know how to handle all of the problems and situations which start popping up, you begin to seek answers by asking advice from others who have been through the same experience. You read books, watch educational videos, talk with experts, and find coaches, trainers, or instructors for guidance on the journey.

At this point you have a choice to make. You can either receive the advice and guidance by putting it into practice or not. Now comes the hard part. It will be an uncomfortable process to make the personal changes necessary in order to continue the journey with positive progress. It will be painful to accept personal weaknesses, and quit blaming others for problems or failures. Through this time of testing you dig deep, finding the discipline it takes to go on. Despite the difficulties at this stage you get the courage to commit to move forward with excellence. As you realize you are not perfect and that only perfect practice makes perfect you begin the hard work it takes to finish the journey.

4. TRUST AND HARD WORK

First you are excited about the new adventure. Then reality sets in and doubts appear. Next you accept you that don't have all the answers so you seek help. After you make the commitment to move forward with excellence you trust the knowledge you have gained from reputable sources. And last, there is no getting around it; you have to work hard at applying everything you have learned in order for it to work. Like step three this is the middle. It is where things seem to go on forever! We think:

Will I ever have this baby? Will this horse ever get it? Will I ever get it? I am getting bored or worse yet frustrated. I am definitely out of my comfort zone and the challenges seem bigger than I can handle. I wonder if I will ever have a breakthrough. Do I really have to keep practicing this until I get it? There has to be an easier way!

5. BREAKTHROUGHS

You are now at the birthing stage. A precious new life is about to be delivered. You are getting close to the ending or culmination of the experience. Something major changes in the relationship with your horse. During this breakthrough there is a moment when your horse acknowledges you in a different way, allowing you into his inner circle. A new partnership is born with your horse.

The amount of effort required at this final stage is much greater than compared to the middle stages. The good thing is it is a much shorter period of time than the middle phase. During this final period those who have been through childbirth know the intensity and pain involved in this labor of love required to complete the delivery. A breakthrough is like this. You are working really hard and all of a sudden it gets even harder. The moment it gets harder you are about to make a major breakthrough which will change your life forever. This is when all the hard work of the middle is paying dividends. A new relationship with respect and trust is finally being developed into a partnership. Sometimes it may seem like you are going backwards. Then all of a sudden, there it is, the birth is complete. The labor pains are over, or so you think.

6. JOY/LOVE/RELATIONSHIP

Finally an ending! The precious little baby lies in the arms of a loving mother looking back. Then the realization comes with excitement: It is another new beginning. The journey of learning continues.

Just when you think you have perfected your horsemanship skills and have arrived at the end of your journey something humbling comes along to remind you that isn't so. For a moment you may let this experience steal the joy, confidence and the relationship you have developed with your horse. **You must not let this happen!** You have to get back on and ride through the pattern again. If you do, you will become an even better horseman.

7. EXCITEMENT ONCE AGAIN!
Go back to the beginning and start the cycle of learning all over again.

No matter where you are on the cycle of learning the **journey continues**. Is there really ever an ending?

Giddy Up, Let's Go

"It is not because things are difficult that we do not dare, it is because we do not dare, things are difficult." – Seneca

My concern for readers of this book is it may make you feel better, but does not get you thinking and working at winning a horse's heart. If this happens then my purpose for writing it has failed. Please do not let this book be a pacifier which substitutes for the process. Allow the information contained herein to apply to you in its entirety. Let it spur you on toward the hard work, courage, conviction, dedication, and the changes it will take to become a horseman who can win the heart of your own chosen horse.

When I take a walk back in my memory of the horses I have encountered, I wish I could go back and apologize to some of them for the way I handled certain situations. My ignorance about how to win a horse's heart wasn't even apparent to me at the time. It wasn't until someone pointed out to me there was a better way that I saw my lack of understanding. I choose to look at the information given to me with an eye of sensitivity to sort out the truth. Then I received these truths with modesty so I could use my comprehension of this information to fill in the holes that were so obvious in my foundation. The decision to do this is an individual choice that each one of us has to make.

One of the most difficult things I have had to learn is that it is not my place to tell folks how to work with their horses unless they ask. It is even more difficult to accept the fact that not all folks will ask. If you have read this book to this point you must be a person who asks questions or at least are curious about learning new things and what others believe. You might not agree with everything I have written, but I hope it has caused you to think about your own principles and beliefs about how to win a horse's heart.

There are a lot of things I see in the horse world which I don't agree with. Even when I witness a situation where I feel the horse isn't getting a fair deal, I try to learn something to improve my own communication by watching with my mouth shut. In many of these situations the person misinterprets the horse's behavior or underestimates the horse's reactions. Sometimes I cringe while observing such a scene. But I still don't judge the person, because they must be doing what they are doing for some reason, even if I don't agree with or understand it. They are probably doing the best they can at this time with the knowledge and experience they have.

Just because I don't like the way a person handles a horse or the fact that we have philosophical differences doesn't give me the right to tell them how I think they should do things, unless they ask. But it does break my heart to watch in silence because I know the horse could offer so much more if he was given half a chance. However, I will intervene if I see someone doing something which will deliberately hurt the horse or a person is in real danger. Even if it means I might not win a popularity contest. We can't impose our philosophy or techniques on anyone unless they are curious, but we can help prevent unnecessary injuries to either the horse or the human.

There is more than one right way to get things done with a horse. In fact there are hundreds of different ways to get things done with a horse. All of them may work, but maybe only ten or so of them are the best deal for the horse. I am seeking those ten effective ways that are the optimum arrangement for the horse which can lead to winning his heart. Not everything suits every horse. That is why reading the horse, focus, feel, timing, and release are essential to being an artisan of horsemanship. This takes years to develop. One or two clinics, watching some DVD's, or reading a few books will not make you a doer of horsemanship. It is a lifetime study involving concentrated devotion to application of everything one learns. Horsemanship is a journey with many twists, turns, and even detours along the way, so we must be diligent to stay focused.

I realize people learn at different paces and we don't all have the same amount of time and energy to put into our growth and learning. Nor do we all have the same goals and dreams. But sometimes we can fall into a rut where even though we have been to clinics, read a lot of books, and watched numerous training videos, our progress isn't as good as we know it could be. Maybe we rely a little too much on the reinforcement, inspiration, motivation, approval, and safety provided by these kinds of learning environments. I am not suggesting any of this is wrong, but it is often hard to sustain the high provided by these settings once we are at home alone with our horse and the reality of life comes rushing in. That is why continuous support is valuable and permanent changes in our life are necessary in order to make the long haul. Getting out there with your horse and using some elbow grease whether it is perfect or not can help guard against falling into a rut.

I am not implying clinics, books, or training videos are not viable ways of learning and gaining knowledge because they are, or I wouldn't have written this book. The process of learning is as varied as the learner. Clinicians, authors of books, and producers of videos all attempt to convey their message in a way which is constructive to the learner. But if we go looking for a magic pill, or one secret which will solve our problems, instead of meaningful principles which can revolutionize our life, then we may still find ourselves unable to progress once the glow wears off after reading a book, watching a video, or attending a clinic.

Why do some people still get stuck in a rut having the same old difficulties with their horses over and over again even after attending clinics, reading books, and watching videos? There are a million different answers to this question, but I believe some of the reasons are fear, frustration, lack of fun, not enough funds, or a missing support system! Any of these excuses can stall out a person until they are crippled and are no longer moving forward. We need to take charge of these justifications. Failure will not be able to overtake us if our determination to succeed is strong enough. Besides determination we need a focus which has scope and depth. Without some kind of set course of action our focus will be fuzzy, our scope and depth shallow, and therefore advancement will be stagnant. A curriculum which is driven by philosophy, theory, research, principles, personal support, and how-to steps with a developmental sequence will supply a clear plan of action which leads to constant improvement.

The sluggish period of wallowing in fear of failure and old ways that don't work must be left behind before winning a horse's heart can become reality. Instead of being trapped by not having appropriate answers, free yourself to find a program with support, or at least develop your own positive plan based on a solid set of principles and stick to it! By sticking to it and not being tossed around by the wind from one opinion to another you will reach your goals much faster. Even with the knowledge of this truth some people may have to go ahead and learn from the school of hard knocks. If someone thinks that is the best route for them, then go ahead. But remember that there is someone out there who has been where you are with your horse and there is help for those who choose to receive it. There are some things in life which maybe only a horse can teach us, and in my experience the difference between giving and receiving could be one of those lessons.

Every person has to solve their own problems, develop their own potential, live their own dreams, find their own feel, and eventually reveal and ride their own horse. A trainer, clinician, book, or video can't always do the work for you. But you can do it!
So mount up, cause we're going' for a ride. Giddy up. Let's go. Let's live our dreams and   win our horse's hearts.

"Even if you're on the right track, you'll get run over if you just sit there." -- Will Rogers

"Trail of Inspiration for the Journey"

Ker plop, plop the rhythm of the three beat gait
sustained in a repetitive chorus sounded in her ears.
She could feel the timing in her body as her muscles moved
with ease in harmony to the beat.
The steady cadence of the pattern offered her
strength and courage for the journey.

There was a moment of suspension in the pattern
where she felt freedom deep in her soul.
It represented a space in time when the world
was in perfect alignment and she found peace.
It was a silent pause in the infinity of time
that lifted her spirit to unimaginable places.

The melody she sang in her heart
could be heard by the wind.
A heart-warming smile on her face
could be seen from the heavens.
The love she poured out spilled onto his mane
and encompassed them both with joy unspeakable.

They were traveling a trail less traveled
which was both perilous and rewarding.
They were living a life long dream
when two hearts beat as one.
The earth beneath them was marked
with an impression of each hoof beat.
They were leaving a trail of *inspiration for the journey*
where enjoying the journey is more important than the final
destination.

- Sherry Jarvis

Robert Browning's "Paracelsus":

Truth is within ourselves; it takes no rise
From outward things, what'er you may believe.
There is an inmost centre in us all,
Where truth abides in fullness; and around,
Wall upon wall, the gross flesh hems it in,
This perfect, clear perception which is truth.
A baffling and perverting carnal mesh
Binds it, and makes all error: and to know
Rather consists in opening out a way
Whence the imprisoned splendor may escape,
Than in effecting entry for a light supposed to be without.

SUMMARY:

"Anything forced and misunderstood can never be beautiful"

> *By Greek soldier Xenophon, who wrote "On Horsemanship" in 350 BC*

The Price We Pay

The minute you purchase a horse you have opened yourself up for a ride of a lifetime. It can either be a dream come true or a nightmare awakened. We know this ride will involves risk, endurance, responsibility, and commitment. Horses deserve better than a half-hearted commitment because they are one of nature's finest creations. We all pay for savvy horsemanship. There isn't a free road to becoming a horseman with true *feel*. You can buy an inexpensive horse, but the road to becoming a great horseman who can win a horse's heart is expensive. The lessons are there for us to learn, if we are willing to pay the price. The price comes in the form of:

Willingness to take risks
100% commitment
Responsibility for decisions
Learning from mistakes
Accountability for the horse's well being
Persistence
Endure discomforts both emotional & physical
Allow for significant character changes
Become a creative thinker with an open mind

Mold an attitude of justice and patience
Overcome fears
Leadership skill development
Physical fitness
Time management
Sacrificing goals to meet the needs of the horse
Listening more carefully
Watching more intently
Discovering effective ways of communication
Preserve the horse's dignity at all cost
Do your foundation homework thoroughly
Dedication to education
Financial sacrifices

How to Win Your Horse's Heart

"Do you wish to rise? Begin by descending. You plan a tower that will pierce the clouds? Lay first the foundation of humility." -- Saint Augustine

Principles to Live By

Stay teachable
Set aside old habits, patterns, beliefs
Be open and honest in self-evaluation
Be willing to make personal changes and try new things
Learn from mistakes
Deal with your fears; learn to control and overcome them
Understand the nature of a horse and how they think
Think, act, speak, and play like a horse
Consider things from horse's point of view
Listen to what horse is trying to communicate
Respect and protect dignity, spirit, and curiosity of horse
Build a horse's strengths instead of focusing on weaknesses
Use positive reinforcement to build respect and trust
Establish and maintain rapport
Discover ways to motivate using safety, comfort, play, food
Take responsibility for physical, emotional, and mental care
of a horse in birth, life and death
Be willing to follow program

Cultivate Important Attitudes:

Positive
Progressive
Patience
Compassion
Empathy

Humility
Desire to grow
Principles before goals
Quit blaming horse
Flexibility
Commitment
Perseverance
Calmness
Consistency
Fairness
Confidence
Balance
Forgiving
Determination

Value Time:

Live in reality of moment
Enjoy the moment
Slow down, take the time it takes
Know when to quit
Realistic time frames for goals
Get on horse time!

Develop Skills:

Be Observant
Read a horse
Think
Problem Solve
Make decisions
Use Common Sense
Timing
Focus
Feel

Visualization
Communication by body language
Make the right things easy
Set realistic plans
Self-Discipline

"What we obtain too cheap, we esteem too lightly." -- Thomas Paine

Recommended Resources to Further the Journey

"Any ideas, plan, or purpose may be placed in the mind through repetition of thought." -- Napoleon Hill

Books to Read
Kinship with All Life by J Allen Boone
7 Habits of Highly Effective People Stephen R. Covey
Animals Make us Human by Temple Grandin
Animal in Translation by Temple Grandin
True Horsemanship Through Feel by Bill Dorrance
True Unity by Tom Dorrance
The Faraway Horses by Buck Brannaman
Lyons on Horses by John Lyons
Natural Horse Care by Pat Coleby
Move Closer Stay Longer by Stephanie Burns
There are No Problem Horses, Only Problem Riders by Mary Twelveponies
The Soul of a Horse Life Lessons from the Herd by Joe Camp
Horses Never Lie by Mark Rashid
Birdie Dr. Deb Bennett

Horsemanship Learning Programs or Clinicians

Parelli Natural Horsemanship
Chris Cox Horsemanship
Richard Winters
Karen Scholl
Brian Newbert
Ray Hunt
Deb Bennett
Leslie Desmond
Karen Rohlf

Martin Black
Carolyn Resnick
JP Giacomini
Dominique Barbier
Walter Zettle
Eitan Beth-Halachmy
Sherry Jarvis with Heart in Your Hand Horsemanship

Magazines

Eclectic Horseman

About the Author

Sherry has always loved horses. She got her first pony "Ginger" when she was only two years old. They grew up together and were riding with their hearts intertwined at a very young age. These two were best friends for over thirty years.

Sherry grew up in a rodeo family, so competition was a big part of the reason for having horses. It seemed that most of the horse people she knew rode their horses to practice for competitions more than for pleasure. Sherry spent a lot of time just hanging out with her horses enjoying their company. She loved riding the pastures, jumping the hay bales in the alfalfa field, swimming the rivers together, and pretending to be a pioneer, a jockey in the Kentucky derby, a rider in the Olympics, or a circus trick rider.

The relationship was always important to her as she sought to win each horse's heart. Winning a big competition didn't seem as satisfying or lasting to her as those rides bareback along the river with the wind blowing freely in her face, feeling the muscles of her steed beneath her, and they became one. What little girl hasn't gained confidence, strength, character, value, responsibility and power from the love relationship with her horse?

After attending college to be trained as a teacher Sherry worked a short while for the Howard Pitzer Ranch near Ericson, Nebraska, riding young horses. It was a great learning experience for her. Even without the knowledge and skills that she has since acquired, the Pitzers thought she was quite handy with horses. That could only be attributed to raw talent, because she still had a lot to learn about the inner workings of a horse and how to win a horse's heart. Through an intense desire to study and learn from a lot of horses Sherry has been able to mold that raw talent into an effective means of communication with horses.

After twenty-five years of working as an educator Sherry has used her training in the mental, physical and emotional factors involved in learning to make available a practical approach to horsemanship which can help ordinary people get extraordinary results with their horses.

When horsemanship clinics started becoming popular in the nineties Sherry discovered the holes in her foundation which had hindered her from turning her raw talent of horsemanship into a harmonious art form. This new-found knowledge inspired her with an even stronger determination and dedication to share with horse lovers the importance of a natural foundation. When you put developing a partnership first with your horse it will change your life. Those positive changes will benefit the life of every horse you encounter and you will also personally profit in many other areas of your life.

Sherry hopes to be instructing students and sharing her passion for mental, physical and emotional fitness for horsemen and their horses all the rest of her days.

The author welcomes correspondence:
Sherry Jarvis
82507 465th Ave.
Burwell, NE 68823

Or send e-mail: sherry @heartinyourhand.com
Visit web site at: www.heartinyourhand.com

www.ingramcontent.com/pod-product-compliance
Lightning Source LLC
Chambersburg PA
CBHW032051080426
42733CB00006B/232